Jump Start Your Career
in Technology & IT
in about 100 Pages

Table of Contents

Chapter 1 Introduction

The technological world has faced many important changes in the latest years. Up until a few years ago, personal computers were the primary and only connection to the digital world: people used them to surf the web, to write documents, to watch videos, to play, and to perform business activities.

Nowadays, personal computers still play an important role, but they are often replaced or used together with new devices—like smartphones and tablets—which open up a new set of scenarios, thanks to their unique features such as long battery life, lightness, hardware sensors, and connectivity.

Windows and Windows Phone are the two key platforms in the Microsoft ecosystem that have been created and evolved to answer to the user's needs in this changing world.

Windows 8.1

Windows 8 has been a game changer in the Microsoft ecosystem: until Windows 7, Windows was primarily a traditional platform dedicated to desktop and notebook computers. Windows 8, instead, introduced a new approach. Thanks to its new Start screen, which replaced the old Start menu, and the new Windows Store apps, the platform has been redesigned to enable a touch experience. The old desktop experience based on mouse and keyboard is still there, so you can still use it; however, the new operating system is also optimized for tablets and a new generation of devices, like Ultrabooks and convertibles, which combine the traditional desktop experience with a touchscreen interface.

Windows 8 has been a game changer for developers too: the new Windows Store apps don't rely anymore on the traditional .NET Framework, which has been the base development platform for many Microsoft technologies in the latest years (like WPF, Silverlight, or ASP.NET). Windows 8, in fact, introduced a new native runtime platform called Windows Runtime, which offers better performance and better support to the latest and most powerful technologies used in modern devices and applications (like movements sensors, geo localization, Bluetooth, etc.).

Windows 8 has also changed the typical lifecycle of a Microsoft operating system. The technological world is changing fast, and the traditional Windows development cycle (with a major release of the operating system every three years and minor Service Packs in between) is not enough to keep up with competitors anymore. With Windows 8, Microsoft is increasing the release frequency; Windows 8.1 is the first outcome of this new approach. Released approximately one year after Windows 8, it added many new features, both for consumers (like new tile formats, a new control panel, better OneDrive integration, etc.) and developers (with 5,000 new APIs, new hardware support, etc.). Some months later, Microsoft updated its operating system again by releasing Windows 8.1 Update 1, which added many features to improve the traditional desktop experience with a mouse and keyboard.

Figure 1: The Windows 8.1 Start screen

Windows Phone 8.1

Windows Phone was one of the first products to showcase the new Microsoft identity. Many of the new concepts introduced with this platform (the flat design, the live tiles, the new development approach, etc.) have become the fundamentals of all the Microsoft products and services that followed, like Windows 8 or the Xbox One. In addition, Windows Phone was the first real consumer product that broke the legacy of the old Windows world. It was the successor of Windows Mobile, but, except for the kernel, it shared nothing with the old platform, from the user experience to the app development approach.

One specific Windows Phone feature is the hardware approach, which takes the best from both Apple's and Google's worlds. Like Google, Microsoft allows multiple vendors to create Windows Phone devices. Thanks to this choice, you can find a great range of phones on the market with different form factors, hardware features, and prices. At the same time, Microsoft has total control over the operating system: vendors can't customize the basic user experience. So regardless of the device the user is going to buy, they'll have access to the same features and to the same interface, making Windows Phone familiar to everyone and easy to recognize. In addition, Microsoft has defined a set of standard hardware requirements that are helpful to developers, who can develop apps without worrying that the phone where the app will run will be missing a basic feature (like the GPS or the accelerometer).

The first Windows Phone version was marked with the 7.0 release number. It was a good start, but it lacked many features compared to the competition, since Microsoft had to start the development of its mobile platform from scratch. Consequently, some months later Microsoft announced Windows Phone 7.5, the first major update, which introduced many new features for both consumers (the task switcher, speech integration, social network integration, etc.) and developers (background execution, database support, etc.).

However, after the Windows Phone 7.5 release, Windows 8 came out and, from a technical point of view, it created a misalignment between the two platforms. Despite the similarities for the user (the flat design, the live tiles, the application's lifecycle, etc.,), there were many differences under the hood. In fact, Windows Phone 7.5 still relied on the old Windows Mobile kernel and on the Silverlight framework for app development.

Windows Phone 8.0 was the first game changer in this scenario: it introduced many important consumer features (a redesigned start screen, new tiles, support to new technologies like NFC, etc.), but more importantly, it started to align the platform with the "big brother," Windows 8. Microsoft replaced the old Windows Mobile kernel with the same Windows 8 kernel, which lead the two platforms to share a common infrastructure, common drivers, and common security features.

Things started to change from a developer's point of view as well: Windows Phone 7.5 apps still relied on the Silverlight framework, but thanks to a special subset of the new Windows Runtime, Microsoft started to introduce some similarities between the two platforms. Consequently, many APIs and features (like storage access, sensors, and Bluetooth) were shared between them, so you were able to achieve the same goal on both platforms by writing the same code.

However, only about 30 percent of the APIs were shared between the two platforms, and many key scenarios (live tiles, application's lifecycle, XAML controls, etc.) were implemented in different ways. Windows Phone 8.1 solved most of these problems: by sharing more than 90 percent of the same APIs, developers are now finally able to write applications for both platforms with a common codebase.

Windows Phone 8.1 is a huge update from a consumer point of view as well, with the addition of important features like Cortana (a digital vocal assistant), the World Flow keyboard, a notification center, better SD card support, and much more. However, the team doesn't rest on their laurels: a few months after the Windows Phone 8.1 announcement, Microsoft released Windows Phone 8.1 Update 1, which introduced many new interesting consumer features, like support to Live Folders, better support for accessories apps (like smart watches or fitness wristbands), improved messaging management, and more.

Figure 2: The Windows Phone 8.1 Start screen

The Windows Store apps

Windows Store apps are a new kind of app, which offers a completely different approach compared to the old traditional desktop apps. The biggest difference is the design and user experience. Instead of relying on the old approach based on Windows, Windows Store apps usually run in full screen and, even though they still support traditional inputs like mouse and keyboards (Windows 8), they are optimized for use with a touch screen.

In addition, the lifecycle is very different, since they're not made just for traditional computers, but also smartphone and tablets. Good performance and low battery consumption are two key factors and, consequently, there are a series of constraints that they need to respect when it comes to memory usage and background execution (we will detail them in Chapter 4).

Other important requirements for mobile apps are stability and security. Tablets and smartphones should always be fast and reactive to the user interaction, and apps shouldn't be able to corrupt the operating system, making the device slow or unsafe to use. For this reason, Windows Store apps run inside a sandbox: they are not allowed to access to the data exposed by other applications or by the operating system, unless the user or application allows it.

Last but not least, Windows Store apps have a unique visual style, called Modern Design, which relies on the following principles:

- **Pride in craftsmanship:** Like a craftsman pays attentions to details during his work, a designer should focus on the right balance of the visual elements and on correctly aligning the various controls placed in the page.
- **Be fast and fluid:** The user interface should be easy to use on a touch screen and should react quickly to the user interaction. This principle also applies to a wise usage of animations: they should be quick and fluid—they don't have to slow down the user experience.
- **Authentically digital:** This is probably the most important and innovative principle of Modern Design, which was introduced first by Microsoft, but today, is one of the most widely used approaches when it comes to software or website design. In the past, the visual design of many software products (websites, mobile operating systems, etc.) was defined using an approach called **skeuomorphism**. Its purpose was to mimic, as close as possible, real world objects. The iOS versions prior to iOS 7 were a good example of this approach: the calendar app was rendered as a real calendar; the notes app was designed as a set of paper sheets, etc. With the passage of time, this approach has started to be less relevant, since it tried to mimic objects that aren't widely used anymore in everyday life. The "authentically digital" approach is the opposite of skeuomorphism: the user interface should be simple and modern, so that the user can immediately understand that he's using a digital product and not an emulation of a real object.
- **Do more with less:** This principle is connected to another important concept, which is "content over chrome." In the latest years, designers tried to fill the visual layout of websites and applications with effects and animations that often distracted the user from the real content. This principle overturned this approach by putting the content at the center of the application: there is still room for effects and animations, but only when they add value for the user, and not when they steal space from the content.
- **Win as one**: This principle is strictly connected to the native Windows and Windows Phone experience, which allows developers to integrate their apps with their operating system and to follow the basic guidelines. This way, users will find themselves at home, no matter which apps they are using.

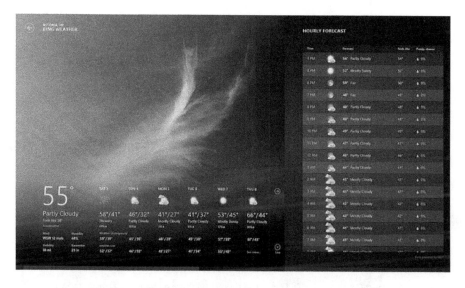

Figure 3: A Windows Store app for Windows 8.1: MSN Weather

The stores

Windows Store apps run in a protected environment and, consequently, they are distributed using a unique channel: the Store. It's a controlled environment: when you publish an application, it goes through a certification process that makes sure that the app follows the technical and security requirements and user experience guidelines outlined by Microsoft. Applications can also be distributed manually, but not in consumer scenarios: manual deployment is supported only for testing and enterprise scenarios.

It's important to note that, at the time of this writing, universal Windows apps still output two distinct binaries, so a Windows Store app for Windows can't run on Windows Phone, and vice versa. Consequently, there isn't a single store, but two different stores, each one distributing only apps for the specific platform they're running on. However, thanks to a shared identity, you'll be able to connect the two versions of your app on the two stores. That way, for example, a user won't have to pay twice if she wants to download both the tablet and phone version of your app. We'll see more details in Chapter 12.

Applications can be published on the stores using a developer account, which can be purchased from Microsoft. It costs $19 for individuals and $99 for companies; both are one-time fees. However, there are two ways to get a free developer account:

- If you're a student, you can get a free token, thanks to a special program called DreamSpark (more details on http://www.dreamspark.com).
- If you're an MSDN subscriber, you can get a free token as part of the benefits with certain subscription types.

Even though there are two stores, the developer account is unique and grants you access to publish apps for both platforms. Thanks to this account, you'll be able to publish both free and paid apps. With paid apps, Microsoft will keep 30 percent of the price of the app, leaving the remaining 70 percent to the developer.

The Windows Runtime

Windows 8 wasn't only a break from the past for users, but also for developers. Windows Store apps, instead of relying on the .NET framework that developers previously used to create desktop and web apps, are based on a new runtime platform called Windows Runtime. It's a native runtime that is built on top of the Windows kernel and offers a set of APIs that apps can use to interact with the hardware and the operating system. It uses a similar approach to the old one, based on COM (Component Object Model), created in 1993 with the goal to define a single platform that could be accessed with different languages.

The Windows Runtime uses a similar approach by introducing **language projections**, which are layers added on top of the runtime that allow developers to interact with the Windows Runtime using well-known and familiar languages, instead of forcing them to learn and use only C++. The available projections are:

- **XAML and C# or VB.NET:** This is the projection that will be more familiar to Windows Phone developers, since it can be used to develop Windows Store apps using C# or VB.NET for the logic, and XAML to define the layout. This projection is implemented with a special subset of the .NET Framework 4.5.
- **HTML and Javascript:** This is the projection that will be appreciated mostly by web developers, since it allows them to use web technologies to create Windows Store apps. The application's layout is defined using HTML 5, while the logic is based on a special library called WinJS, which grants access to the Windows Runtime APIs using JavaScript.
- **XAML and C++**: This projection can be used to create native applications using a C extension called C++ / CX, which makes easier to developers to interact with the Windows Runtime using C++.
- **C++ and Direct X**: This projection is especially useful for games, since it allows developers to create native applications that make use of all the powerful features offered by the DirectX libraries to render 2D and 3D graphic.

The Windows Runtime libraries are described using special metadata files, which make it possible for developers to access the APIs using the specific syntax of the language they're using. This way, projections are able to respect also the language conventions and types, like uppercase for C#, or camel case for JavaScript.

The Windows Runtime support has been added in Windows Phone 8.0, with a specific subset called **Windows Runtime for Windows Phone**. However, as I already mentioned, only about 30 percent of the APIs were shared between Windows and Windows Phone. Windows Phone 8.1 introduced an almost full implementation of the Windows Runtime by sharing not only 95+ percent of the APIs, but also the Windows Store apps concept and model.

This book is focused on the XAML and C# projection; even if the described APIs and features are available to any projection, the code samples will be only in XAML and C#.

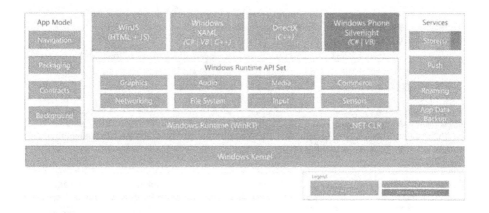

Figure 4: The Windows Runtime architecture

Universal Windows apps

Windows Phone, prior to the 8.1 release, relied heavily on the Silverlight framework: even if the Windows Runtime was there and some APIs were shared between the two platforms, in most cases, creating an app for Windows and for Windows Phone was a very different experience. In fact, many fundamental concepts (like navigation, the application lifecycle, and the visual controls), despite the similarities, were implemented in a different way, making it more complex for developers to share code among the two platforms.

With Windows Phone 8.1, things have changed. With an almost full convergence between the two platforms, now you can create Windows Store apps both for Windows and Windows Phone, which can share most of the code, assets, and visual controls. Universal Windows apps can also share the same identity, which means that data, purchases, and roaming settings can be shared across multiple devices.

However, there is one important thing to highlight: Windows Store apps for Windows and Windows Phone still output two separated binaries, which are distributed using two different stores. Windows Store apps for Windows can't run on Windows Phone, and vice versa. Consequently, the "Universal Windows app" concept doesn't define a real application, but it refers to a specific Visual Studio template that allows code to easily be shared between the two versions of the same application. As we'll learn in the next chapters, Universal Windows app templates are composed by three projects: one for Windows, one for Windows Phone, and one shared, where you can include all the assets, classes, and visual controls that you want to share among the two platforms.

Silverlight for Windows Phone 8.1

If you are already a Windows Phone developer, you'll find many differences in Windows Store apps compared to Windows Phone Silverlight applications. Even if the base concepts are the same, there are many key scenarios that are implemented in a different way (like navigation or application's lifecycle) or with different APIs (like push notifications, tiles management, and network operations).

Consequently, if you have already developed a Windows Phone application and you want to convert it into a Windows Store app, Visual Studio doesn't offer a way to do it automatically. Due to the many breaking changes in layout controls and APIs, it's an operation that can only be performed manually, by rewriting the layout or the code that uses controls and APIs that aren't available anymore.

Since this approach would require all the Windows Phone developers to rewrite the existing apps, Microsoft found a way to keep the compatibility with the Silverlight framework and, at the same time, allow use of most of the new features added in Windows Phone 8.1. **Silverlight for Windows Phone 8.1** is an updated version of Silverlight, which guarantees compatibility with the codebase of your existing app. This way, you'll be able to target Windows Phone 8.1 simply by upgrading your project in Visual Studio, which will give you access to the new APIs and features. You won't have to change the existing code—all the old Silverlight APIs will continue to work just fine. However, this approach has a downside: you won't be able to use the Universal Windows app template, since, under the hood, you'll still have to deal with a Silverlight app. Consequently, sharing code between a Windows Store app for Windows and a Silverlight app for Windows Phone isn't as easy as with a Windows Store app for Windows Phone.

For this reason, this book will focus only on Windows Store apps and the Universal Windows app template. You'll be able to use most of the features and APIs described in the book in a Silverlight app, but when it comes to the fundamental concepts (like navigation, application lifecycle, and layout controls) you'll find a reference only to the Windows Store apps approach.

If you want to know more about Silverlight apps, you can download my previous Syncfusion book, *Windows Phone 8 Development Succinctly,* from http://syncfusion.com/resources/techportal/ebooks/windowsphone8.

Windows vs. Windows RT

When you work with smartphone apps, you typically don't have to worry about the CPU architecture: all the Windows Phone devices on the market are based on ARM, a CPU architecture very commonly used in the smartphone market, due to its good performance and the low battery consumption. Consequently, all the apps distributed on the Windows Phone Store are compiled for the ARM processor architecture.

However, when it comes to Windows, things are different: Windows 8 is an operating system that targets both tablet and traditional computers. While typically tablets are based on ARM, traditional computers are based on the x86/x64 architecture, made popular by companies like Intel and AMD.

Consequently, Microsoft has created two different versions of the operating system: Windows 8, which runs on x86/x64 processors, and Windows RT, which runs on ARM processors. The first one is the traditional Windows version, which offers full support both to the new Windows Store apps and to the traditional desktop with all the existing apps. You can find it both on traditional computers and on tablets. Thanks to the work made by Intel with the latest processors, hardware manufacturers like Asus or Dell have created tablets that run the full version of Windows and offer, at the same time, good performance and battery life.

Windows RT, instead, is a special Windows version made for tablets. At first sight, it looks like the full Windows version, but because of the different architecture, traditional desktop apps won't run (except for the ones provided directly by Microsoft, like a special Office 2013 version, which is preinstalled); only Windows Store apps can be executed. The biggest advantage of the Windows RT version is that it's more consumer friendly: since traditional X86 apps and processes can't run, the platform is basically invulnerable to malwares and viruses, so it's safer to use for people with little computer knowledge. Microsoft has created its own device, which runs Windows RT, called Surface (not to be confused with the Surface Pro, a full-powered PC the size of a tablet that runs the full Windows version).

In most cases, developers won't have to worry about the CPU architecture; the Windows Store apps compiled by Visual Studio can run on both architectures without any change. The only exception is when you need to use native libraries in your project: native code can't be compiled for both architectures, so you'll need to create two different versions of the app. The Store will take care of distributing the proper one according to the user's device. We'll more about this approach in the next chapters, when we'll need to use some native libraries like SQLite.

What's next? Windows 10

Microsoft has launched a Technical Preview version of their next operating system, Windows 10. How this release will impact the application development is still unknown: the main focus of the Technical Preview is to provide a glimpse of all the new features that are being added to the platform to win back the traditional desktop users who were skeptical about the new operating system approach (the new Start screen menu, full screen applications, etc.). Some of the new features are:

- A redesigned Start screen, which combines the best of the Windows 7 and Windows 8 approaches: it's a traditional start screen menu, but with the ability to display live tiles from Windows Store apps.
- The ability to run Windows Store apps in a window that can be resized like a traditional desktop app.
- Improvements to better separate the touch experience from the traditional mouse experience. For example, the charms bar and the old Start screen are now displayed only if the user is interacting with the touch screen of the device.

When the first Technical Preview was released at the end of September, Microsoft clearly stated that Windows 10 will be the fundamental core of all its upcoming products: Windows, Windows Phone, Xbox One, etc. Consequently, in the future we can expect a tighter integration and an improved convergence of the Windows Runtime that runs on every platform, and the Store experience.

Figure 5: The Windows 10 convergence across multiple devices

The development tools

The tool to develop Windows Store apps for Windows and Windows Phone is **Visual Studio 2013**, which is available in multiple versions:

- The Community Edition, which can be downloaded from http://www.visualstudio.com/en-us/products/visual-studio-community-vs. It's a completely free version with the same features offered by the Professional version. It can be used by individual developers, students, open source project developers, and small companies.

- Different paid versions that can be purchased from Microsoft or in bundle with a MSDN subscription. In this case, you will need to install at least the Update 2, which adds support for Universal Windows apps and Windows Phone 8.1.

In terms of the Windows Store apps development experience, you won't find any difference or limitation in the Community version: you'll be able to create and publish apps in the same way you can with a professional Visual Studio version. If you're a student, you can also check the DreamSpark program (https://www.dreamspark.com/), which allows you to get all the Microsoft professional tools for free.

Visual Studio 2013 is focused on developing apps for Windows 8.1 and Windows Phone 8.0 and 8.1. If you need to work on apps for the previous versions of the operating system (like Windows 8.0 or Windows Phone 7.8), you will need Visual Studio 2012. However, this book is focused on Universal Windows apps for Windows 8.1 and Windows Phone 8.1, so you won't find any detail on previous versions.

The minimum hardware requirements are a Windows 8.1 computer with a 1.6 GHz processor, 1 GB of RAM, and at least 4 GB of free space on the hard disk. If you are planning to use the Windows Phone emulators, you will also need:

- A Professional or Enterprise Windows 8.1 64-bit version.
- A processor that is able to support SLAT, which is a hardware chip that is required by Hyper-V, the Microsoft virtualization technology developed by Microsoft used to run emulators. The post published at http://blogs.msdn.com/b/devfish/archive/2012/11/06/are-you-slat-compatible-wp8-sdk-tip-01.aspx will show you how to find out if your CPU supports this feature.
- At least 4 GB of RAM (8 GB are suggested if you're planning to run multiple emulators at the same time).

Testing your apps

Windows 8.1

There are three ways to test a Windows 8.1 app using Visual Studio.

- By deploying the application on the PC you're using for development. Since it's a Windows 8.1 computer, Windows Store apps will run just fine. However, to improve the testing experience, it's strongly advised to have a touchscreen computer or monitor: this way, you can test the app's usability both with touch and mouse/keyboard.
- Using the integrated simulator: this approach launches a dedicated simulator that opens a remote desktop session on your own computer (you'll notice that you'll find the same apps and the same visual settings of your current computer). The simulator is useful to test scenarios that are hard to verify on a real computer, thanks to a set of additional tools like:
  o Touch gestures: By using the mouse, you'll be able to simulate different touch gestures, like pinch to zoom, or rotation touch.
  o Rotation: It's used to simulate the device's rotation in portrait or landscape mode.

- o Resolution: You'll be able to simulate different resolutions and screen sizes, to check that the layout of your application properly behaves on every device.
- o Location: This tool can be used to insert a specific set of geographic coordinates, which will be sent to the application.
- o Network properties: You can simulate different types of network connections, like Wi-Fi or roaming.
- By deploying the app on another device, like a Windows RT tablet: Microsoft has released an application called **Remote Tools for Visual Studio 2013** (http://s.qmatteoq.com/RemoteTools), which is available both for ARM and X86 devices, that needs to be installed on the tablet you want to use for testing. Thanks to this tool, you'll be able to deploy and debug the application as if it's installed on your current PC.

Windows Phone 8.1

Visual Studio 2013 includes a set of different Windows Phone emulators, which are based on the Microsoft virtualization technology called Hyper-V. They aim to recreate a real Windows Phone device, and they can access your computer's hardware. For example, if you have a touchscreen, you can use it to simulate the phone's screen; or if you have a microphone, you can use it to simulate the phone's internal microphone.

Since Windows Phone devices come with different resolutions and screen sizes, you'll find multiple emulators available in Visual Studio 2013 to simulate different kind of devices.

In addition, Windows Phone emulators offer a set of utilities that can be accessed from the **Additional tools** section:

- **Accelerometer:** It can be used to simulate the movement of the device in 3D-space, so that you can test apps that make use of the accelerometer sensor.
- **Location:** With help of a map, you can simulate the phone's position and send the coordinates to the emulator. This way, you'll be able to easily test applications that use the geolocation APIs.
- **Screenshot:** This tool can take a screenshot of the current screen in the emulator. It's especially useful when you are ready to submit your app to the Store, since part of the required info is at least one screenshot of the application.
- **Network**: This section can be used to change the type of network connectivity, so that you can simulate a slow connection or poor signal.
- **SD Card**: Thanks to this feature, you can simulate that an SD card is inserted into the phone, so that you can test the dedicated APIs that allow you to read and write data from an external memory. We'll detail them in Chapter 5.
- **Notifications**: It's used to simulate push notifications, so that you can test how your app is able to react when one of them is received, even if your notifications backend isn't ready yet. We'll go into detail about notifications in Chapter 10.
- **Checkpoints**: Every time you close the Windows Phone emulator, its state is automatically reset; when you open it again, you'll find the original state restored. With this feature, you'll be able to save the current state (installed apps, storage data, current regional settings, etc.), so that it can be restored for later usages.
- **Sensors:** This section can be used to customize the number of sensors that are available on the device; this way, if your app is using one of them, you can test that you are correctly managing the scenario where your app is running on a device without that specific sensor.

Of course, Windows Phone applications can be tested on real devices: in fact, it's advised to always test an application on a device before submitting it to the store, since performance can be very different from the one offered by the emulator. However, to improve security and to mitigate piracy, you can't simply deploy an application to the phone: all the apps need to be installed from the Store. Since this approach can create problems when it comes to testing an application, developers are allowed to unlock their devices, so that they can deploy up to 10 applications directly from Visual Studio and debug them like you can do with the emulator.

This goal is achieved using a tool installed together with Visual Studio 2013, called **Windows Phone Developer Registration 8.1**. Once you've opened it, you'll have to connect your device to the PC using the USB cable and log in with your Microsoft account. If everything goes well, the device will be unlocked and you'll be able to manually deploy your applications. If something goes wrong, you'll receive a detailed message that will explain the reason. Some common errors are:

- Both the device and the computer should be connected to Internet.
- You have already registered the maximum number of allowed devices.
- The date and time on your phone should be correct.

If your Microsoft Account is linked to a developer account (the one that gives you the rights to publish an app to the Store), you'll be able to unlock up to three devices; otherwise, you can unlock just one device. However, at any time you can connect to your dashboard on the Windows Phone Dev Center and remove the unlocked devices you don't use anymore to free spots for new phones.

Figure 6: The Windows Phone 8.1 emulator

Using NuGet

NuGet is a popular package manager that simplifies the developer's life. When it comes to adding a third party library to our project, instead of browsing the web, searching for it, and then downloading and manually adding a reference in our project, we can use NuGet to perform all these operations for us. NuGet will take care of downloading the library, adding a reference to the proper DLL (or DLLs), and setting up the project with all the required files and configurations.

We're going to use NuGet in many scenarios in this book to install third-party libraries that can simplify our job. Using NuGet is really simple: right-click on your project and choose the **Manage NuGet packages** option. You will a see the NuGet main window, which you can use to find new packages on the core repository, uninstall an already installed package, or update an existing one. You can also access an option called **Manage NuGet packages for Solution** by right-clicking on the solution. In this case, you'll be able to manage the packages that are installed on every single project, which is particularly useful for Universal Windows apps, since you have to deal with at least two different projects (one for Windows and one for Windows Phone).

To add a package, it's enough to search for it by name or by keyword: after you've found it, just click on the **Install** button that is displayed near the package description. NuGet will take care of everything for you.

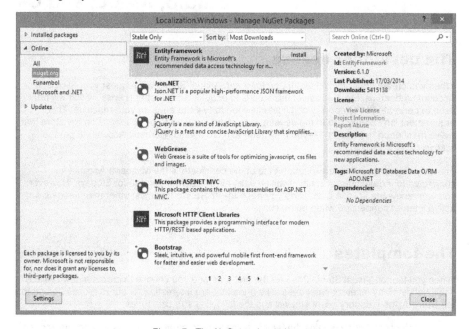

Figure 7: The NuGet main window

Chapter 2 The Essential Concepts: Visual Studio, XAML, and C#

The developer license

When you create your first Universal Windows app, Visual Studio will request your Microsoft Account credentials: the purpose of this step is to acquire a developer license, which will be used to generate the temporary certificate needed to test the apps on your machine. This requirement isn't connected to the developer account required to publish apps on the store that we've mentioned in Chapter 1—you only need to have a valid Microsoft Account to get the license.

The only difference is in the expiration date of the certificate: if the Microsoft Account is connected to a developer account, it will be valid for 90 days, otherwise for 30 days. However, you can renew the license every time you need to—there are no limits, other than needing an active internet connection when doing so.

The templates

When you launch Visual Studio 2013 for the first time and you choose to create a new project, you'll notice many different categories. The ones that are interesting for our purposes belong to the **Store Apps** category. Here you will find the following sub categories:

- **Universal Apps** contains the templates needed to create a Universal Windows app, so it will create a shared project, plus a project for each platform.
- **Windows Apps** contains the templates needed to create a Windows Store app just for Windows 8.1.
- **Windows Phone Apps** contains the templates needed to create a Windows Store app just for Windows Phone. In this category, you'll find also some templates with the suffix **Windows Phone Silverlight**: they can be used to create a phone app based on the Silverlight framework, both for Windows Phone 8.0 and 8.1.

If you create an application just for Windows or Windows Phone, and you change your mind later, you can turn it into a Universal Windows App anytime: just right-click on the solution in the Solution Explorer window to add the project for the other target.

Whichever template you choose to create a Universal Windows app, Visual Studio will create for you a solution composed of three projects:

- One with the **.Windows** suffix, which contains the Windows Store app for Windows 8.1
- One with the **.WindowsPhone** suffix, which contains the Windows Store app for Windows Phone 8.1
- One with the **.Shared** suffix, which contains all the data (code, XAML controls, assets, etc.) that you want to share between the two platforms.

Shared projects are managed with a technique called **linked files**: every time you add a file to the shared project, a link will be automatically added to the specific projects for the two platforms. Consequently, Visual Studio will compile all the files inside the specific package, bundling them together, but the shared file will physically exist in only one location. This way, when you edit the file, the changes will be automatically available to both projects.

Pages, XAML, and code behind

Windows Store apps abandon the old window-paradigm to use a new window based on pages, which are organized in a hierarchical way. After launching the app, the user lands on the main page; from there, he can move to the other pages, which contain different and specific content. For example, a news application can display the list of the most recent news in the main page. The user can tap one of them and navigate to a detail page, which will display the full text of the news. In addition, the application can have more pages: one for videos, one for photo galleries, one for a specific news category, etc.

All the pages inside an application are composed of two different files:

- The main file, which ends with the **.xaml** extension. It contains the visual layout of the page and is written with a language called XAML, which is based on XML.
- The code behind, which ends with the **.xaml.cs** extension. It contains the code that is able to interact with the user interface and perform logic operations. To see this file in Solution Explorer, you'll have to click on the little arrow that is displayed near the XAML file. In fact, the code-behind file is displayed as a child of the XAML file in the tree structure. The language used in the code behind depends on the projection you're using: in our samples, it will contain C# code.

The project's structure

Regardless of the template you use, there are some files and folders that are essential for a Windows Store app and included in every project. Let's look at the most important ones.

The App.xaml file

Initially, you may think of this file as representing one of the application pages: in fact, like any other page, it's composed by an XAML and a code-behind file. Actually, the App.xaml file is a special class, since it (usually) is the starting point of every Windows Store app. It takes care of initializing everything needed by the application to properly work, starting with the Frame class that manages the different pages of the application. In addition, it offers all the entry points to manage the application's lifecycle, which will be detailed in Chapter 4.

One important feature of the **App** class is that its instance is kept alive until the app is closed or suspended: every property that is declared in this class can be accessed for later usage when the application is running. Another consequence of this behavior is that the App.xaml file is the central point where you register all resources (like styles and templates), which can be used from the controls placed in the application's pages. We'll see in detail how to use this feature later in this chapter.

The Assets folder

This folder typically contains all the visual assets (images, logos, icons, etc.) that are used in the application. It's not a strict requirement: you can place such data in any other folder of the project. However, it's a good practice to place everything in the Assets folder. Visual assets can be placed in the shared project, but by default, they are created in the specific projects for Windows and Windows Phone. The reason is that often the two applications—even if they display the same data—need to use different images, due to the different form factors and resolutions supported by tablets and smartphones. However, in the next chapters, you're going to see that Windows Store apps support a way to easily manage the different resolutions and device sizes. Thanks to a feature called bundling (which will be detailed in Chapter 12), you'll be able to include all your images in the shared project and let the phone automatically download the proper images during the installation from the Store, according to the device where the application is running.

The manifest file

Inside every platform's specific project, you'll find a special file called **Package.appxmanifest**. It's called the **manifest file**, and it's very important: its purpose is to define all the main features of the application, like the standard visual assets (logos, tiles), the metadata (name, description), the capabilities, the integration with operating system, etc. Under the hood, it's an XML file, but Visual Studio provides a visual editor, which is automatically loaded when you double-click on it.

The manifest is composed of the following sections:

- **Application:** This section describes all the base metadata of the application, like the name, the default language, the supported orientations, and the push notifications configuration.
- **Visual assets**: This section describes the visual layout of the application, by defining all the default images that are used as logos for the Store, as backgrounds for the default tile, or as splash screens to display when the application is being loaded. Since Windows and Windows Phone support multiple resolutions and screen sizes, this section will allow you to upload different formats for the same image. In Chapter 4, you'll better understand how Windows and Windows Phone manage this scenario.
- **Requirements**: This section is available only on Windows Phone, and it lists a set of hardware features that our application may use (like the gyrometer or the camera). This way, users with devices without these features won't be able to install the application from the Store.
- **Capabilities**: This section is used to set up which features (hardware or software) the application is using, like the internet connection, the geolocation services, the picture

library, etc. In this book, you'll find a special note every time we cover a feature that requires you to enable a specific capability.

- **Declarations**: This section is used to extend the application so that it can deeply interact with the operating system or with other applications. Every time we're going to use some code that extends the applications (like performing operations in background or sharing a content), we'll need to set up the entry points in this section. We'll detail this section in the final chapters of the book, when we talk about contracts and background execution.
- **Content URIs**: This section is specific for a control called **WebView**, which can be used to display web content inside the application (like an HTML page). This control offers developers a way to interact with the page, by intercepting and calling specific JavaScript functions. This feature is enabled only for trusted websites, for which URLs needs to be added in this section. To improve security, only sites that use the HTTPS protocol are supported.
- **Packaging**: This last section can be used to customize some information about the package that you will publish on the Store, like the application name, the publisher name, or the version number. Much of the information detailed in this section is automatically set when you associate your app with the Store to publish it; you'll find more details in Chapter 12.

The XAML

XAML stands for **Extensible Application Markup Language**: it's based on XML, and it's used to define the visual layout of a page, in a similar way that HTML is used to define the layout of web pages.

Controls (like buttons or a block of text) are identified by an XML tag, which is inserted inside a page following a hierarchical structure. Tags can be inserted inside other tags to define a relationship. For example, this approach is widely used to define the layout of the page: there are some special controls (which we'll detail in Chapter 3) that act as container for other controls and, consequently, they are nested one inside the other.

Here is what a page definition looks like:

```xml
<Page
    x:Class="Styles.MainPage"
    xmlns="http://schemas.microsoft.com/winfx/2006/xaml/presentation"
    xmlns:x="http://schemas.microsoft.com/winfx/2006/xaml"
    xmlns:local="using:Styles"
    xmlns:d="http://schemas.microsoft.com/expression/blend/2008"
    xmlns:mc="http://schemas.openxmlformats.org/markup-compatibility/2006"
    mc:Ignorable="d">

    <Grid>
        <StackPanel>
            <TextBlock Text="Hello world" />
        </StackPanel>
    </Grid>
</Page>
```

Every page inherits from a base class called `Page`, which is the starting node; every other tag placed inside it will define the page layout. You can see that in the page definition there's an attribute called `x:Class`: it defines which code-behind class is connected to the page. In the sample, it's a class called `MainPage`, which belongs to a namespace called `Styles`.

Namespaces

The concept of namespaces should already be familiar to developers: it's a way to better organize your code by defining a logical path for your classes. This way (even if it's not a suggested approach), you can also have two classes with the same name, given that they belong to two different namespaces. Namespaces are separated using a period; if, for example, you have a class called `Person`, which belongs to the `Entities` namespace, it will be represented by the full definition `Entities.Person`. Usually, by default, namespaces inside a project are mapped with folders: if you create a folder called `Entities` and you create a new class inside it, by default it will belong to the `Entities` namespace.

Namespaces in XAML behave in the same way: XAML controls are, in the end, standard classes, which belong to a specific namespace. When you want to use a control inside a page, you have to make sure that the proper namespace is added in the page definition. This is true especially for custom controls created by the developer or for third-party controls that are included in external libraries. In fact, most of the native controls (buttons, textboxes, etc.) can be used without having to worry about the namespace.

Let's see an example about how to use a namespace in XAML with the Bing Maps control, which is an external library that can be added in a Windows Store app for Windows to display a map. This control is included in the namespace `Bing.Maps`; consequently, you'll need the following declaration in the `Page` definition:

```
xmlns:maps="using:Bing.Maps"
```

Every namespace starts with the `xmlns` prefix (XML Namespace), which is always required. Then, you need to specify a unique identifier for the namespace, which will be used inside the page every time you need to get access to a control or a class that belongs to it (in the previous sample, it's `maps`). Here is the sample code to display the Bing Maps control inside a page:

```
<maps:Map x:Name="MyMap" />
```

As you can see, we've added as prefix to the name of the control (`Map`) the identifier we've previously assigned to the namespace (`maps`).

Properties and events

Every control can be customized in two ways: by defining properties, and by subscribing to events. Each of them is identified with an attribute of the control, even if they have two different purposes.

Properties are used to determine the control's aspect and behavior, and are set simply by assigning a value to the specific attribute. Let's say that we want to display text on the page by using a control called **TextBlock**: in this case, we'll need to change the value of a property called **Text**, like in the following sample.

```
<TextBlock Text="Hello world" />
```

However, there are some properties that can't be expressed with a simple string like in the previous sample. For example, if you want to define an image as background of a control, you need to set a property called **Background** using the extended syntax, like in the following sample:

```
<Grid>
    <Grid.Background>
        <ImageBrush ImageSource="/Assets/Background.png" />
    </Grid.Background>
</Grid>
```

The extended syntax is expressed with a node that is set as child of the control: the prefix is the same of the control's name, followed by name of the property separated by a period. In the example, since we need to set the **Background** property of a control called **Grid**, we use the expression **Grid.Background**.

There's a special property that is offered by any control, called **x:Name**: it's a string that univocally identifies it in the page (you can't have two controls with the same name). It's especially important because it allows developers to access to the control from the code behind: thanks to this identifier, you'll be able to read and set properties directly from the code.

For example, let's say you have a **TextBlock** control and you assign to it a unique identifier in the following way:

```
<TextBlock x:Name="MyText" />
```

You'll be able, in the code behind, to interact with the control simply by using the value of the **x:Name** property. The following sample shows how to change the **Text** property in the code:

```
MyText.Text = "Hello world!";
```

Events, on the other hand, are used to determine how the user or the application is interacting with your control. Every time something happens that involves the control, an event is raised, and you'll be able to manage it in the code behind. A very common event is **Click**, which is exposed by all the controls that offer a direct interaction with the user, like the **Button** control. Every time the user presses the button (either with a click of the mouse or with a tap), the **Click** event is raised. You will need to manage it with a specific method, called an **event handler**. Visual Studio will help you to define this method in the proper way: after you write the event's name you want to assign to the event, Visual Studio will take care of creating the event handler in the code for you.

The following sample shows you how to define an event handler for the `Click` event of a `Button` control in XAML:

```
<Button Click="OnButtonClicked" />
```

Visual Studio will generate the following event handler:

```
private void OnButtonClicked(object sender, RoutedEventArgs e)
{
    MyText.Text = "Hello world!";
}
```

As you can see, event handlers are regular methods, but with a specific definition: they always offer some parameters (usually two) that, as developer, we can use to better track the event. The first parameter is called the **sender** and, it's a reference to the object that invoked the event (in our sample, it will contain a reference to the `Button` control). The second parameter, instead, offers some properties that are useful to understand the event context. We'll see more detailed sample usages of this parameter in the next chapters. Inside the event handler, you simply need to write the code that you want to execute when the event is raised. In the previous sample, we set the `Text` property of our `TextBlock` control every time the `Button` is pressed.

Visual Studio offers a feature called **IntelliSense**, which is able to autocomplete the code while you're writing and offer some useful information about properties and events on the fly. IntelliSense also offers a useful visual reference to distinguish properties and events: properties are identified by a small wrench, and events by a lightning bolt.

Figure 8: The different icons used to highlight properties and events

Resources

If you've ever worked with web technologies like HTML, the resources concept will be familiar to you. As in the HTML world, you are able to share and reuse styles in multiple pages by using CSS files. Resources can be used to define a control's style and behavior, and to reuse it in different pages of the application.

Resources are defined by a property called **Resources**, which is offered by any control. Since XML is based on a hierarchical structure, every nested control will be able to use the resources defined by its parent. The following example shows how to define some resources that will be available to a **Grid** control and to any other control nested within it:

```
<Grid>
    <Grid.Resources>
        <!-- insert here your resources -->
    </Grid.Resources>
</Grid>
```

However, resources are more often defined with two different scopes: page and application.

Page resources are defined within the page itself, thanks to the **Resources** property that is offered by the **Page** class. This way, all the controls that are included in the page will be able to access to the resources. Here's an example of a page resources definition:

```
<Page
    x:Class="Styles.MainPage"
    xmlns="http://schemas.microsoft.com/winfx/2006/xaml/presentation"
    xmlns:x="http://schemas.microsoft.com/winfx/2006/xaml"
    xmlns:local="using:Styles"
    xmlns:d="http://schemas.microsoft.com/expression/blend/2008"
    xmlns:mc="http://schemas.openxmlformats.org/markup-compatibility/2006"
    mc:Ignorable="d">

    <Page.Resources>
        <!-- insert here your resources -->
    </Page.Resources>
</Page>
```

Application resources, instead, are defined using the **Resources** property of the **Application** class that is defined in the **App.xaml** file. This way, the resources will be available to any control placed in any page of the application. Here is a sample definition:

```
<Application
    x:Class="Styles.MainPage "
    xmlns="http://schemas.microsoft.com/winfx/2006/xaml/presentation"
    xmlns:x="http://schemas.microsoft.com/winfx/2006/xaml"
    xmlns:local="using:Styles">

    <Application.Resources>
        <!-- insert your resources here -->
    </Application.Resources>

</Application>
```

Like controls are univocally identified by the **x:Name** property, resources are identified with the **x:Key** property. To apply a resource to a control's property, you need to use a special XAML syntax called **markup extension**: it's a way to describe, directly in XAML, complex operations that would otherwise require writing some logic in code. There are many markup extensions available in XAML, and we'll talk about some of them during this chapter.

The one that is used to apply a resource to a control is called **StaticResource**. Here's an example of how to use it to apply a style to a **TextBlock** control:

```
<TextBlock Style="{StaticResource CustomStyle}" />
```

The resource is applied by including the **StaticResource** keyword inside braces, followed by the name of the resource (which is the value assigned to the **x:Key** property).

In some cases, especially if you have a lot of resources, the page or the application's definition can be become too crowded and hard to read. XAML offers you a way to better manage resources, by declaring them in a dedicated file, in the same way that in HTML you can define CSS styles in another file and not just inline.

In XAML, these external files are called **Resource Dictionaries**. Visual Studio offers a specific template to create such files: just right-click on your project in Solution Explorer and choose **Add > New Item**. You'll find, as one of the available templates, a file's type called **Resource Dicitonary**. Automatically, it will create a file with the following definition:

```
<ResourceDictionary
    xmlns="http://schemas.microsoft.com/winfx/2006/xaml/presentation"
    xmlns:x="http://schemas.microsoft.com/winfx/2006/xaml">

    <!-- here you can place all your resources -->

</ResourceDictionary>
```

Using this file is really easy: you just have to include, inside the **ResourceDictionary** tag, all your resources, just like you did when you added them as page or application resources. Then you need to include the Resource Dictionary file inside the main application by declaring it in the App.xaml file in the following way:

```
<Application.Resources>
    <ResourceDictionary>
        <ResourceDictionary.MergedDictionaries>
            <ResourceDictionary Source="Resources/Styles.xaml" />
        </ResourceDictionary.MergedDictionaries>
    </ResourceDictionary>
</Application.Resources>
```

Resource dictionary files are added inside the `MergedDictionaries` property, offered by the `ResourceDictionary` class. In the previous sample you can see that we've added just one file, but you can add as many as you want (if, for example, you want to split resources in different files, according to their type or use case).

Let's see now, in detail, which kind of resources the XAML framework offers to developers.

Styles

Styles in XAML are very similar to CSS styles: their purpose is to collect multiple property definitions in one style, so that when the style is applied to a control, all the properties are automatically changed. This way, if you change your mind and you want to edit one of the properties, you can do it in just one place (the style definition), instead of manually editing all the controls.

Here's how a style looks:

```
<Style TargetType="TextBlock" x:Key="RedStyle">
    <Setter Property="Foreground" Value="Red" />
    <Setter Property="FontSize" Value="30" />
</Style>
```

Styles are identified by the **Style** control, which offers a property called **TargetType** that is used to specify which kind of controls this style can be applied to. Inside the **Style** control you can place as many **Setter** tags as you want: each one is able to change the value (using the **Value** attribute) of a specific property (using the **Property** attribute).

In the previous sample, we defined a style that can be applied just to **TextBlock** controls and changes two of its properties: the color (**Foreground**), and the text size (**FontSize**).

Styles can be applied to any control with a type that matches the one we've defined in the **TargetType** property. This way, you won't have to manually apply the style using the **StaticResource** property; it will be automatically applied. These styles are called **implicit styles**, and they are defined simply by omitting the **x:Key** property, like in the following sample:

```
<Style TargetType="TextBlock">
    <Setter Property="Foreground" Value="Red" />
    <Setter Property="FontSize" Value="30" />
</Style>
```

All the **TextBlock** controls will automatically display the text using a bigger font, in red. Implicit styles are applied based on the scope where they've been defined: if they've been declared in a page, they will be automatically applied to all the controls in the page; otherwise, if they've been declared as an application's resources, they will be applied to all the controls in all the pages.

It's important to remember the hierarchical nature of XAML: in the case of styles, it means that inner styles always win over outer styles. If, for example, you have defined a page style that changes the **TextBlock**'s color in red, but then you manually apply another style that changes the color in blue, the last one will win over the generic one.

Data templates

Data templates are special resources that can be applied to some controls in order to define the visual layout. They are often used in combinations with controls that are used to display collections of items, like `ListView` or `GridView`, which we'll cover in Chapter 3.

The data template simply contains the XAML that is used to render each item of the list, and the XAML will be automatically repeated and applied to every element of the list. Let's say that you want to display a list of people; here's how your data template might look:

```
<DataTemplate x:Key="PeopleTemplate">
    <StackPanel>
        <TextBlock Text="Name" />
        <TextBlock Text="{Binding Path=Name}" />
        <TextBlock Text="Surname" />
        <TextBlock Text="{Binding Path=Surname}" />
    </StackPanel>
</DataTemplate>
```

For now, just ignore the `Binding` keyword; it's a new markup extension, which will be covered in detail later in the chapter. For the moment it's important just to know that, with this data template, you'll be able to display the name and surname for every person in the collection.

Data templates behave like any other resource: they can be defined inline inside the control, as page or application's resource, or in a resource dictionary. Then, you can apply them using the `StaticResource` keyword. Typically, when you're dealing with controls to display collections, data templates are assigned to a property called `ItemTemplate`, which defines the template used for each item in the collection:

```
<ListView ItemTemplate="{StaticResource PeopleTemplate}" />
```

Brushes

Brushes are XAML elements that are used to define how a control is filled. For example, when you set the background color of a `Button` control, you're using a brush. There are many kind of brushes: the simplest one is called `SolidColorBrush`, and it's used to express a color. Most of the time, you'll be able to apply this brush using the standard property's syntax. It's enough to assign the color's name to the required property, since the XAML runtime will take care of creating a `SolidColorBrush` for you under the hood. For example, you could create a `Rectangle` shape with a red background:

```
<Rectangle Width="200" Height="200" Fill="Red" />
```

There are also more complex brushes that can only be expressed with the extended syntax. For example, you can apply a gradient instead of a simple color by using a `LinearGradientBrush` or a `RadialGradiantBrush`. They both have the same purpose, but while `LinearGradientBrush` uses a line as a separator between the colors, `RadialGradiantBrush` applies a circular effect.

Here is how you can apply a gradient brush to the same **Rectangle** control we've seen before:

```
<Rectangle Width="200" Height="200">
    <Rectangle.Fill>
        <LinearGradientBrush>
            <GradientStop Color="Blue" Offset="0" />
            <GradientStop Color="Red" Offset="1" />
        </LinearGradientBrush>
    </Rectangle.Fill>
</Rectangle>
```

Inside a gradient brush, we can insert multiple **GradientStop** controls; each of them defines one of the colors that will be applied. With the **Offset** property, you can specify the location where the gradient stops. Optionally, you can also apply the **StartPoint** and **EndPoint** properties to define the points where the gradient should start and end.

In the end, you can also apply an image as a brush by using an **ImageBrush** control, which also requires the extended syntax:

```
<Rectangle Width="200" Height="200">
    <Rectangle.Fill>
        <ImageBrush ImageSource="background.png" />
    </Rectangle.Fill>
</Rectangle>
```

Handling resources based on the theme

So far, we've seen just one way to apply resources to a control: by using the **StaticResource** keyword. However, the Windows Runtime improvements added in Windows and Windows Phone 8.1 include a new keyword, called **ThemeResource**, which can be used to automatically adapt a resource according to the device's theme.

Let's take a step back and see in detail how this feature works: both Windows 8.1 and Windows Phone 8.1 offer support to different themes. In Windows, they're connected to the accessibility (Ease of Access) settings. In the Control Panel, users can enable one of the high contrast themes, which can be useful for people with visual handicaps. In Windows Phone 8.1, themes are part of the native user experience: the user can enable, in the phone's settings, the **dark theme** (white text on black background) or the **white theme** (dark text on white background).

Developers need to keep in mind this feature when it comes to designing an application; otherwise, there's the risk that it will work properly with just one of the themes, making it unusable with the other ones.

Let's say you have a **TextBlock** control in the page and you force the text's color to white: a user with the white theme on the phone won't be able to read it. Thanks to the **ThemeResource** keyword, you'll be able to define multiple resources with the same name, and the system will automatically apply the one that works best for the current theme.

Here an example:

```
<Application.Resources>
    <ResourceDictionary>
        <ResourceDictionary.ThemeDictionaries>
            <ResourceDictionary x:Key="Dark">
                <SolidColorBrush Color="Red" x:Key="ApplicationTitle" />
            </ResourceDictionary>
            <ResourceDictionary x:Key="Light">
                <SolidColorBrush Color="Blue" x:Key="ApplicationTitle" />
            </ResourceDictionary>
        </ResourceDictionary.ThemeDictionaries>
    </ResourceDictionary>
</Application.Resources>
```

As you can see, we've defined (as application resources) two resources with the same name: they're both **SolidColorBrush** controls, and they have the same **x:Key** value, which is **ApplicationTitle**. However, the two brushes have a different purpose: the first one sets the color to **Red**, the second one to **Blue**.

Both have been added inside a **ResourceDictionary** property called **ThemeDictionaries**: an important difference is that each **ResourceDictionary** has a unique identifier, assigned with the **x:Key** property. This identifier tells the system which theme the resources are referred to, by using a specific naming convention:

- **Default**, which is applied as default's theme.
- **Dark**, which is applied when the dark theme is used.
- **Light**, which is applied when the light theme is used.
- **HighContrast**, which is applied when the high contrast theme is used.

Now you just need to apply your resource as you did before, but using the **ThemeResource** markup extension instead of the **StaticResource** extension. Here's a sample that shows you how to apply the previous style to a **TextBlock** control:

```
<TextBlock Text="Title" Foreground="{ThemeResource ApplicationTitle}" />
```

One of the most useful advantages of this markup extension is that it's able to detect the theme change at runtime: this way, if the user changes the theme while the app is running, all the resources will be automatically adapted, without having to restart the app.

You can also force a theme for your application, by applying the **RequestedTheme** property to the whole application (in the App.xaml file), or to a single page or control. This way, the resources will ignore the user's theme and follow only the rules defined by the forced theme. The following sample shows how to force the entire application to use the **Dark** theme:

```
<Application
    x:Class="Qwertee.App"
    xmlns="http://schemas.microsoft.com/winfx/2006/xaml/presentation"
    xmlns:x="http://schemas.microsoft.com/winfx/2006/xaml"
    xmlns:local="using:Qwertee"
    RequestedTheme="Dark">
```

```
</Application>
```

Animations

Animations are probably one of the most powerful resources in XAML: with a few lines of XAML code, you'll be able to animate virtually any control in the page. For instance, you can make a control disappear, move to another position, or change in size.

Animations are rendered using a control called **Storyboard**, which offers different types of animations:

- **DoubleAnimation** is used when you want to animate the control by changing a numeric property (like the **FontSize**).
- **ColorAnimation** is used when you want to animate the control by changing a color property.
- **PointAnimation** is used when you want to animate the control by changing its coordinates.

Before seeing in detail how an animation works, let's see a code sample that defines a **DoubleAnimation**:

```
<Storyboard x:Name="Animation">
    <DoubleAnimation Storyboard.TargetName="MyShape"
                     Storyboard.TargetProperty="Opacity"
                     From="1.0"
                     To="0.0"
                     Duration="0:0:5" />
</Storyboard>
```

Attached properties are special properties that are inherited from a control, but that can be applied to other ones. In this case, **TargetName** and **TargetProperty** are two attached properties: they are exposed by the **Storyboard** control, but they're applied to the **DoubleAnimation** control. Their purpose is to define where the animation will be applied: **TargetName** defines the name of the control, while **TargetProperty** the name of the property, which value will be changed during the animation.

In the previous sample, we're changing the **Opacity** property of a control identified by the name **MyShape**. The other three properties define the behavior of the animation: **From** and **To** are used to define the starting and ending value of the property, while **Duration** is used to express the animation's length. In this case, we're changing the **Opacity**'s value of the control from 1.0 to 0.0; the animation will last five seconds. After five seconds, the control will disappear.

With the previous code, the animation is equally distributed according to the specified length. XAML offers a way to change this behavior by using one of the controls that ends with the suffix **UsingKeyFrames**. The following sample shows another approach to defining a **DoubleAnimation**:

```
<Storyboard x:Name="Animation">
```

```
<DoubleAnimationUsingKeyFrames Storyboard.TargetName="MyShape"
                               Storyboard.TargetProperty="Opacity"
                               Duration="0:0:10">
    <LinearDoubleKeyFrame KeyTime="0:0:3" Value="0.8" />
    <LinearDoubleKeyFrame KeyTime="0:0:8" Value="0.5" />
    <LinearDoubleKeyFrame KeyTime="0:0:10" Value="0" />
</DoubleAnimationUsingKeyFrames>
</Storyboard>
```

We're using the alternative version of the control, called **DoubleAnimationUsingKeyFrames**. The difference is that, this time, using the **LinearDoubleKeyFrame** control and the **KeyTime** property, we specify the animation timings exactly. In the sample, the final result is the same (the control disappears after 10 seconds), but with different timings: after three seconds the **Opacity** property will be set to 0.8; after eight seconds to 0.5; and in the end, after 10 seconds, it's set to 0; making the control disappear.

Easing animations

There are some kinds of animations that are pleasant to see for the user, but that can be hard to implement. Let's say you have a shape in the page and you want to simulate that it's falling down towards the bottom of the screen; when the shape touches the bottom margin, it should bounce like a ball. These kind of animations can be complex to define, since they require taking in consideration the laws of physics, like acceleration and gravity.

The XAML framework offers some built-in animations, called **easing animations**, that can be used to implement such behaviors without dealing with all the complexity. Let's see how to implement the bouncing sample using one of these animations:

```
<Storyboard x:Name="EasingAnimation">
    <PointAnimation From="0,0" To="0, 200" Duration="0:0:3"
                    Storyboard.TargetName="Circle"
                    Storyboard.TargetProperty="Center">
        <PointAnimation.EasingFunction>
            <BounceEase Bounces="2" EasingMode="EaseOut" />
        </PointAnimation.EasingFunction>
    </PointAnimation>
</Storyboard>
```

In this case, rather than defining the animation in the regular way (in this sample, it's a **PointAnimation** that moves a shape from one position of the screen to another), we set the **EasingFunction** property with one of the many built-in easing animations available. In the previous sample, we're using a **BounceEase** control, which can be used to add a bouncing effect to the control. Every easing animation offers a set of specific properties to customize it. For example, the **BounceEase** control offers a property called **Bounces** to define how many bounces the control should perform at the end of the animation.

You can see a list of all the available easing functions in the MSDN documentation: http://s.qmatteoq.com/Easing.

System animations

The Windows Runtime offers a built-in set of animations that cover many common scenarios (like fade in or fade out effects). You can identify them by their **ThemeAnimation** suffix. Using these animations is really simple: you just have to add the control in a **Storyboard** tag. In the previous samples, we've seen how to manually apply a fade out effect to a control, by changing the **Opacity** property from 1 to 0. We can achieve the same result using a built-in animation called **FadeOutThemeAnimation**, like in the following sample:

```
<Storyboard x:Name="Fade" TargetName="MyShape">
    <FadeOutThemeAnimation />
</Storyboard>
```

You can see a list of all the available system animations here:
http://s.qmatteoq.com/ThemeAnimations.

Controlling the animations

Animations are defined as resources, like styles and data templates. The only difference is, instead of using the **x:Key** property to identify them, we need to use the **x:Name** property, in the same way we do for regular controls. Here is a sample of an animation defined as page resource:

```
<Page
    x:Class="BLEConnection.MainPage"
    xmlns="http://schemas.microsoft.com/winfx/2006/xaml/presentation"
    xmlns:x="http://schemas.microsoft.com/winfx/2006/xaml"
    xmlns:d="http://schemas.microsoft.com/expression/blend/2008"
    xmlns:mc="http://schemas.openxmlformats.org/markup-compatibility/2006"
    mc:Ignorable="d">

    <Page.Resources>
        <Storyboard x:Name="Animation">
            <DoubleAnimation Storyboard.TargetName="MyShape"
                Storyboard.TargetProperty="Opacity"
                From="1.0"
                To="0.0"
                Duration="0:0:5" />
        </Storyboard>
    </Page.Resources>

</Page>
```

Thanks to the unique identifier, we are able to control the animation in the code, in the same way we are able to interact with the controls placed in the page. The **Storyboard** controls offer some methods to play, stop, or resume the animation. The following sample shows two event handlers connected to the **Click** event, which are exposed by two buttons that are used to start (with the **Begin()** method) and stop (with the **Stop()** method) the animation:

```
private void OnStartClicked(object sender, RoutedEventArgs e)
{
```

```
    Animation.Begin();
}
private void OnStopClicked(object sender, RoutedEventArgs e)
{
    Animation.Stop();
}
```

Transitions

Transitions are not very different from animations, but instead of being able to be executed at any time, they are performed only when a specific event happens (e.g. a page is loaded, or an element in a collection is deleted). The Windows Runtime offers native support to transitions: instead of manually defining the animation, we will simply need to define which one to use, by using the **Transitions** property that is offered by any control. Unlike with animations, we won't need to setup a **Storyboard**, since we don't control the execution.

Here is an example of transitions usage:

```
<Button Content="Transition test">
    <Button.Transitions>
        <TransitionCollection>
            <EntranceThemeTransition />
        </TransitionCollection>
    </Button.Transitions>
</Button>
```

The **Transitions** property accepts a **TransitionCollection** element: its purpose is to support multiple transition effects, in case you want to manage multiple events (for example, you want to apply both an entrance and an exit transition). In this sample, we've applied only an entrance effect, by using the **EntranceThemeTransition** control.

As usual, since we're working with XAML, transitions are propagated to every element nested inside a control. If, for example, we had applied the **EntranceThemeTransition** to a **Grid** control, every other control placed inside it would inherit the entrance animation.

Another scenario where transitions are often applied are collections. For example, you can have animation applied to every single item when the page is loaded, or when an item is removed or added to the list. This scenario is implemented in the same way we've seen for standard controls; the only difference is that, this time, instead of using the **Transitions** property, we use the **ItemContainerTransitions** property, which is supported by any control that is able to display collections of data. Transitions assigned to this property will be automatically applied to every item in the list. The following sample shows this behavior using an **ItemsControl** control:

```
<ItemsControl x:Name="People">
    <ItemsControl.ItemContainerTransitions>
        <TransitionCollection>
            <EntranceThemeTransition />
            <AddDeleteThemeTransition />
```

```
            </TransitionCollection>
        </ItemsControl.ItemContainerTransitions>
</ItemsControl>
```

Most of the advanced Windows Runtime controls offer built-in support to transitions. For instance, the previous sample (a collection of items with a transition effect applied when the items are deleted, added, or displayed in the page) is automatically implemented by controls like **GridView** or **ListView**, which will be covered in Chapter 3.

Visual states

Most of the XAML controls support the concept of **visual state**: a control can assume many states and each of them can have a different visual representation. Let's take as an example a **Button** control: by default, it's displayed with a black background and white text. If you press it, its state changes: the background becomes white, and the text becomes black.

Visual states are an easy way to define the different states without having to rewrite, from scratch, the layout of the control for each state. In fact, each control has a base state, plus a set of other visual states that are expressed by defining the differences with the original state. In the previous sample, the base template of a **Button** will contain the whole definition of the control: the visual stated related to the "pressed" state, instead, will simply change the background and the text's color of the original template.

Let's see an example by adding a couple of **TextBlock** controls to a page:

```
<Grid>
    <StackPanel>
        <TextBlock Text="Text 1" x:Name="FirstText" />
        <TextBlock Text="Text 2" Visibility="Collapsed" x:Name="SecondText"
/>
        <Button Content="Change state" Click="OnChangeVisualStateClicked"
/>
    </StackPanel>
</Grid>
```

When the page is loaded, the first **TextBlock** is visible, while the second one is hidden, since the **Visibility** property is set to **Collapsed**. Our goal is to reverse this situation and to make the first **TextBlock** disappear, while making the second one visible. Here is how we can achieve this result without writing any code, just by using XAML and the visual states:

```
<Grid>
    <VisualStateManager.VisualStateGroups>
        <VisualStateGroup>
            <VisualState x:Name="Default" />
            <VisualState x:Name="ChangedState">
                <Storyboard>
                    <ObjectAnimationUsingKeyFrames
Storyboard.TargetName="FirstText"
```

```
Storyboard.TargetProperty="Visibility">
                          <DiscreteObjectKeyFrame KeyTime="0"
Value="Collapsed" />
                    </ObjectAnimationUsingKeyFrames>
                    <ObjectAnimationUsingKeyFrames
Storyboard.TargetName="SecondText"

Storyboard.TargetProperty="Visibility">
                          <DiscreteObjectKeyFrame KeyTime="0" Value="Visible"
/>
                    </ObjectAnimationUsingKeyFrames>
                </Storyboard>
            </VisualState>
        </VisualStateGroup>
    </VisualStateManager.VisualStateGroups>
    <StackPanel>
        <TextBlock Text="Text 1" x:Name="FirstText" />
        <TextBlock Text="Text 2" Visibility="Collapsed" x:Name="SecondText"
/>
        <Button Content="Change state" Click="OnChangeVisualStateClicked"
/>
    </StackPanel>
</Grid>
```

We've defined a **VisualStateManager**, which offers a property called **VisualStateGroup**:
inside it we can define the different visual states we want to manage in the page. In this sample,
we've created two states: one called **Default**, and one called **ChangedState**. The first one
includes an empty definition: it's the base state, which simply displays the controls as they've
been defined in the page. The second state, instead, contains a **Storyboard** with a set of
animations. The first state is applied to the first **TextBlock** and changes the **Visibility**
property to **Collapsed** to hide it. The second one, instead, is applied to the second **TextBlock**
and changes the **Visibility** property to **Visible**, so that it can be displayed.

Once we've defined the visual states, we need to trigger them according to our requirements:
one way is to do it in code behind, using the **VisualStateManager** class, like in the following
sample:

```
private void OnChangeVisualStateClicked(object sender, RoutedEventArgs e)
{
    VisualStateManager.GoToState(this, "ChangedState", true);
}
```

If you remember the previous XAML definition, we've inserted a `Button` control: when it's pressed, the previous event handler is invoked to trigger the visual state change. The goal is achieved by using the `GoToState()` method offered by the `VisualStateManager` class. It requires three parameters: the control that is going to change its state (typically, it's defined inside the same page, so it's enough to use the this keyword), the name of the state to apply, and a `Boolean` parameter, which tells to the `VisualStateManager` whether or not to apply an animation when the state changes.

The example we've just seen is a very simple one, but visual states are very useful, especially when you have to deal with complex controls. By using the Visual Studio designer or Blend (an XAML designer tool that comes with Visual Studio), you are able to redefine a control's visual states: just right-click on it and choose **Edit template** > **Create a copy**. The tool will generate a copy of all the default styles applied to the control, including one called `Template`, which contains the list of all the available visual states. If you try to perform this operation on a `Button` control, you'll find many visual states that the control can assume, like `Pressed` or `Disabled`.

Data binding

Data binding is one of the most powerful XAML features, and it's crucial to learn it if you want to get serious with Windows and Windows Phone development. Data binding is a way to create a communication channel between the user interface and a data source (which can be a control or a property in the code). In addition, the XAML framework offers a notification mechanism, connected to data binding, that is able to create a real time channel: every time something changes on one side of the channel, the other side is automatically notified and updated.

When you set up a binding, you create a communication channel that involves a **source** (the data source) and a **target** (the control in the user interface that is going to display the data to the user). As default behavior, the channel is created in `OneWay` mode: when the source changes, the target is automatically updated, but not otherwise. Binding is defined using a specific markup extension, called `Binding`, as shown in the following sample:

```
<TextBlock Text="{Binding Path=Name}" />
```

In this case, the source is specified inside the markup extension, using the `Path` attribute (in the previous sample, it's a property called `Name`). The target, instead, is the property which binding is assigned to (in this case, the `Text` one). Specifying the `Path` attribute is optional. The following code works in exaclty the same way:

```
<TextBlock Text="{Binding Name}" />
```

Binding also offers a way to create a two-way communication channel. For example, the `TextBox` control can be used not only to display text, but also to receive text as input from the user. In this case, we want not only for changes from the code to be reflected in the user interface, but also to be able to access user input from the code. To support this scenario, we need to explicitly set the `Mode` property of the binding, like in the following sample:

```
<TextBox Text="{Binding Path=Name, Mode=TwoWay}" />
```

Almost all the XAML controls are able to use data binding. Most of their properties, in fact, are defined as dependency properties, which are special properties that, in addition to offering the standard mechanism to read and write their values, support notifications propagation.

Let's see an example to better understand this concept. Look at the following code snippet:

```
<StackPanel>
    <Slider x:Name="Volume" />
    <TextBlock x:Name="SliderValue" Text="{Binding ElementName=Volume,
Path=Value}" />
</StackPanel>
```

In this sample, we've connected the **Text** property of the **TextBlock** control to the **Slider**: we're always using the **Binding** markup extension, but with a different approach. Instead of just using the **Path** attribute, we added first the **ElementName** attribute. This way, we can refer to another control in the page. In this case, we refer to the **Value** property of the **Slider** control, which contains the slider's value. Both **Value** and **Text** are dependency properties, so they can propagate notifications when something changes. The result will be that every time the user moves the slider on the screen, the **TextBlock** will automatically update itself to display the slider's value.

Data binding with objects

One of the most powerful data binding features is the ability to connect visual controls to objects in our code. This approach is the base of many important XAML concepts and patterns, like Model-View-ViewModel. To explain it, first we need to introduce a new XAML property, called **DataContext**: its purpose is to define the binding context of a control, and like many other XAML features, it's hierarchical. As soon as you define a control's **DataContext**, every other nested control will get access to the same binding context.

Let's see an example: we'll display the info about a person using the data binding approach, instead of manually setting the **Text** property of a **TextBlock** control. The info is stored in a class, which contains some basic info (name and surname):

```
public class Person
{
    public string Name { get; set; }
    public string Surname { get; set; }
}
```

Here is, instead, the XAML we're going to use to display such information on a page:

```
<StackPanel x:Name="Customer">
    <TextBlock Text="Name" />
    <TextBlock Text="{Binding Path=Name}" />
    <TextBlock Text="Surname" />
    <TextBlock Text="{Binding Path=Surname}" />
</StackPanel>
```

As you can see, name and surname are displayed using data binding: the two properties of the **Person** class are connected to the **TextBlock** control using the **Binding** markup expression. Let's see now how to create a **Person** object and display it using this new approach:

```
public MainPage()
{
    InitializeComponent();
    Person person = new Person();
    person.Name = "Matteo";
    person.Surname = "Pagani";
    Customer.DataContext = person;
}
```

When the page is created, we define a new **Person** object and set it as **DataContext** of the **Customer** control, which is the **StackPanel** that contains the **TextBlocks** used to display name and surname. By doing this, we've defined, as binding context of the **StackPanel**, the **Person** object we've just created; now we are able to access to the **Name** and **Surname** properties using binding.

The INotifyPropertyChanged interface

The previous code has a flaw: unlike the example we saw with the **Slider** control, if you change one of the properties of the **Person** class at runtime, during the app's execution, the **TextBlock** controls won't update themselves to display the new value. This happens because **Name** and **Surname** are simple properties and not dependency properties. If you want to enable notification's propagation support, the Windows Runtime offers a specific interface, called **INotifyPropertyChanged**, which you have to implement in your classes.

Let's see how the **Person** class definition we've previously seen changes to properly support this interface:

```
public class Person : INotifyPropertyChanged
{
    private string _name;
    private string _surname;
    public string Name
    {
        get { return _name; }
        set
        {
            _name = value;
            OnPropertyChanged();
        }
    }
    public string Surname
    {
        get { return _surname; }
        set
        {
```

```
                _surname = value;
                OnPropertyChanged();
        }
    }
    public event PropertyChangedEventHandler PropertyChanged;
    protected virtual void OnPropertyChanged([CallerMemberName] string
propertyName = null)
    {
        PropertyChangedEventHandler handler = PropertyChanged;
        if (handler != null) handler(this, new
PropertyChangedEventArgs(propertyName));
    }
}
```

Thanks to the **INotifyPropertyChanged** interface, we are able to define an event called
PropertyChanged, which is raised by the **OnPropertyChanged()** method. Every time we call it,
we notify to the user interface that the property's value has changed.

The second step is to change the properties definition. They can't be simple properties
anymore, because we need to invoke the **OnPropertyChanged()** method every time the value
changes; we do it in the setter of the property.

Now the notification's mechanism offered by data binding will properly work. If you change the
person's name or surname while the app is running, you'll correctly see the new values in the
user interface.

Data binding and collections

Data binding plays a key role when you have to deal with collections of data; every control that
is able to display a collection implements a property called **ItemsSource**, which contains the
data to show in the page.

We've already seen, previously in this chapter, how to define a **DataTemplate** and how to use it
with collections. Whenever you assign a set of data to the **ItemsSource** property, under the
hood you're setting, as **DataContext** of the **ItemTemplate**, the single item that belongs to the
collection.

Let's see an example with a **ListView** control, which uses, as **ItemTemplate**, the
DataTemplate we've previously seen:

```
<ListView x:Name="People" >
    <ListView.ItemTemplate>
        <DataTemplate>
            <StackPanel>
                <TextBlock Text="Name" />
                <TextBlock Text="{Binding Path=Name}" />
                <TextBlock Text="Surname" />
                <TextBlock Text="{Binding Path=Surname}" />
            </StackPanel>
        </DataTemplate>
    </ListView.ItemTemplate>
```

```
        </ListView.ItemTemplate>
</ListView>
```

And here is how we assign a collection of data to the **ListView** control in code:

```
public MainPage()
{
    InitializeComponent();
    List<Person> people = new List<Person>
    {
        new Person
        {
            Name = "Matteo",
            Surname = "Pagani"
        },
        new Person
        {
            Name = "Angela",
            Surname = "Olivieri"
        }
    };

    People.ItemsSource = people;
}
```

Since the collection is assigned as **ItemsSource** of the **ListView** control, the **DataContext** of the **ItemTemplate** becomes the single **Person** object. Consequently, we're able to display the values of the **Name** and **Surname** properties using binding.

Another important Windows Runtime feature when it comes to managing collections and data binding is the **ObservableCollection<T>** class. It behaves like a regular collection, but under the hood, it implements the **INotifyPropertyChanged** interface. Consequently, every time the collection changes (a new item is added or removed, the items order changes, etc.), the control that is connected to it will automatically reflect the new changes visually.

It's important to highlight that the **ObservableCollection<T>** class is able to notify only collection changes. If you want to also notify when one of the properties of the items in the collection changes, you still need to manually implement the **INotifyPropertyChanged** interface in your class.

Converters

Sometimes you might want to change some data in your application before displaying it on the page. A common example is when you have to deal with a **DateTime** object: if you want to display a list of news, it's probably enough to display the simplified date of the news, and not the full representation with hours, minutes, seconds, and milliseconds.

Converters are special classes that are able to satisfy this requirement: they intercept the source data before it is sent to the target control. To properly work, these classes need to implement the **IValueConverter** interface, like in the following code sample:

```
public class DateTimeConverter : IValueConverter
{
    public object Convert(object value, Type targetType, object parameter,
string language)
    {
        if (value != null)
        {
            DateTime date = (DateTime)value;
            return date.ToString("g");
        }
        return string.Empty;
    }

    public object ConvertBack(object value, Type targetType, object
parameter, string
    language)
    {
        if (value != null)
        {
            DateTime date = DateTime.Parse(value.ToString());
            return date;
        }
        return DateTime.Now;
    }
}
```

By implementing the **IValueConverter** interface, you'll be forced to define two methods:
Convert() is the one that is invoked when the source data is intercepted and it needs to be
modified before sending it to the target. The **ConvertBack()** method, instead, is invoked in the
opposite scenario: when the target needs to send the data back to the source. This method is
invoked only when you define a two-way binding; otherwise, you'll need to implement only the
Convert() method.

Both methods will receive, as input parameters, some information needed to perform the
conversion; the most important is **value**, which contains the source data. Since binding can be
applied to any object, the **value**'s type is a generic **object**: you'll have to properly cast to the
type you're working with, according to your scenario.

The previous sample is referred to the **DateTime** scenario we've previously introduced: the
Convert() method takes care of returning the date, while the **ConvertBack()** method takes
the input string and converts it back into a **DateTime** object.

Converters are managed like regular resources: they need to be defined in the **Resources**
property offered by controls, pages, or the application itself. Then, you can apply them using the
StaticResource markup extension to the **Converter** attribute in the binding expression. The
following sample shows how to declare the previous declared converter as a resource, and how
to apply it to a **TextBlock** control:

```
<Page
```

```
    x:Class="SampleProject.MainPage"
    xmlns="http://schemas.microsoft.com/winfx/2006/xaml/presentation"
    xmlns:x="http://schemas.microsoft.com/winfx/2006/xaml"
    xmlns:d="http://schemas.microsoft.com/expression/blend/2008"
    xmlns:mc="http://schemas.openxmlformats.org/markup-compatibility/2006"
    mc:Ignorable="d">

    <Page.Resources>
        <converters:DateTimeConverter x:Key="DateConverter" />
    </Page.Resources>

    <TextBlock Text="{Binding Path=BirthDate, Converter={StaticResource
DateConverter}}" />

</Page>
```

If you want to add a parameter (which will be assigned to the object with the same name in the **Convert()** or **ConvertBack()** method), you just need to add a **ConverterParameter** property to the markup extension, like in the following sample:

```
<Page
    x:Class="SampleProject.MainPage"
    xmlns="http://schemas.microsoft.com/winfx/2006/xaml/presentation"
    xmlns:x="http://schemas.microsoft.com/winfx/2006/xaml"
    xmlns:d="http://schemas.microsoft.com/expression/blend/2008"
    xmlns:mc="http://schemas.openxmlformats.org/markup-compatibility/2006"
    mc:Ignorable="d">

    <Page.Resources>
        <converters:DateTimeConverter x:Key="DateConverter" />
    </Page.Resources>

    <TextBlock Text="{Binding Path=BirthDate, Converter={StaticResource
DateConverter}, ConverterParameter=ShortDate}" />

</Page>
```

It's important to highlight that converters shouldn't be abused: they can have a negative impact on performance, since the converter's logic needs to be invoked every time the binding expression changes. In more complex cases, it's better to directly modify the original property or to define a new property in the class to hold the value to display.

The DataTemplateSelector

Sometimes converters are used when you want to change the visual state of a control according to the data (for example, you want to hide or display it, or to change the text's color). However, due to the potential performance issues mentioned before, this approach isn't always the best solution, especially if you need to deeply change the layout based on data.

For these scenarios, the Windows Runtime has introduced a new approach called **DataTemplateSelector**, which is a special class that is able to return a different **DataTemplate** according to our needs. This way, we won't have to create a layout with lot of converters; we'll simply define two (or more) different templates, and according to our needs, the proper one will be used to render the data.

To see how this feature works, let's change the **Person** class we've seen before, by adding a new property called **Gender**, which will tell us if the person is a male or a female:

```
public class Person
{
    public string Name { get; set; }
    public string Surname { get; set; }
    public char Gender { get; set; }
}
```

Our goal is to display a list of people with a different template according to the gender. The background will be blue in case of a male person, and pink if she's a female. To do this, we need to create a class that inherits from **DataTemplateSelector**, which will define the available **DataTemplate** objects and the condition that will be used to decide which one to apply. Here is a full sample:

```
public class PeopleTemplateSelector : DataTemplateSelector
{
    public DataTemplate MaleTemplate { get; set; }

    public DataTemplate FemaleTemplate { get; set; }

    protected override DataTemplate SelectTemplateCore(object item,
DependencyObject container)
    {
        Person person = item as Person;
        if (person != null)
        {
            if (person.Gender=='M')
            {
                return MaleTemplate;
            }
            else
            {
                return FemaleTemplate;
            }
        }
        return base.SelectTemplateCore(item, container);
    }
}
```

In our scenario, we're going to use two templates. Consequently, the class defines two different **DataTemplate** objects: one for the male template and one for the female template. By implementing the **DataTemplateSelector** class, we are forced to define the **SelectTemplateCore()** method, which is invoked at runtime when the binding is performed. It's the method that will tell to the control that displays the data collection which template to use. For this purpose the method receives, as input parameter, the current item of the collection as a generic **object**. The first step is to cast it to the type we're working with (in our case, the **Person** class). Then we can check the condition we're interested in and return the proper **DataTemplate**. In our sample, we check the value of the **Gender** property: if it's equal to **M**, we return **MaleTemplate**, otherwise we return **FemaleTemplate**.

So far, we've defined just the logic of the **DataTemplateSelector**. Now we need to define the visual layout by specifying how the two templates will look. To do this, we simply define two **DataTemplates** as resources, as we normally would:

```
<Page.Resources>
    <DataTemplate x:Key="MaleTemplate">
        <StackPanel Width="300" Background="LightBlue">
            <TextBlock Text="{Binding Path=Name}" />
            <TextBlock Text="{Binding Path=Surname}" />
        </StackPanel>
    </DataTemplate>

    <DataTemplate x:Key="FemaleTemplate">
        <StackPanel Width="300" Background="Pink">
            <TextBlock Text="{Binding Path=Name}" />
            <TextBlock Text="{Binding Path=Surname}" />
        </StackPanel>
    </DataTemplate>
</Page.Resources>
```

In our sample, the two templates are basically the same, except for the background color applied to the **StackPanel** control. Now we need to define, as resource too, the **DataTemplateSelector** object we've previously created:

```
<Page.Resources>
    <DataTemplate x:Key="MaleTemplate">
        <StackPanel Width="300" Background="LightBlue">
            <TextBlock Text="{Binding Path=Name}" />
            <TextBlock Text="{Binding Path=Surname}" />
        </StackPanel>
    </DataTemplate>
    <DataTemplate x:Key="FemaleTemplate">
        <StackPanel Width="300" Background="Pink">
            <TextBlock Text="{Binding Path=Name}" />
            <TextBlock Text="{Binding Path=Surname}" />
        </StackPanel>
    </DataTemplate>
    <local:PeopleTemplateSelector x:Key="PeopleTemplateSelector"
```

```
      MaleTemplate="{StaticResource MaleTemplate}"
      FemaleTemplate="{StaticResource FemaleTemplate}" />
</Page.Resources>
```

If you remember, in the **DataTemplateSelector** class, we've defined a property for each **DataTemplate** we need to manage. Now we simply need to tell, for each property, which **DataTemplate** to use. Since they are resources, we use the **StaticResource** markup extensions, as we would with any other resource.

The last step is to assign the **DataTemplateSelector** to the control we're going to use to display the data collection. We can do it by using the **ItemTemplateSelector** property exposed by most of the collections' controls. The following sample shows how to do it using a **GridView** control:

```
<GridView ItemTemplateSelector="{StaticResource PeopleTemplateSelector}" />
```

As you can see, we don't need to define the **ItemTemplate** property in this case; the **DataTemplateSelector** object we've created will take care of assigning the proper **ItemTemplate** to every item, according to the logic we've written.

Sharing code in a Universal Windows app

As we've already highlighted in the beginning of this book, Universal Windows apps don't define a real type of application; rather, they're special Visual Studio templates that make it easier to share code between the Windows 8.1 and Windows Phone 8.1 versions of your application. Inside the shared project, you're able to define classes, visual assets, XAML controls, etc. You can also share entire pages of the applications. If you try to define a page inside the shared project and then, from both applications, you trigger the navigation towards this page, you'll notice that the operation will work just fine.

However, this isn't the best approach: even if the two platforms shares a lot of similarities, they still offer a different user experience, due do the different form factor of a tablet or a computer compared to a smartphone. Here is a series of different approaches that, as developers, you can use to maximize the code sharing, while at the same time, defining a different user interface according to the platform.

Partial classes

Partial classes, introduced in the .NET framework, provide a way to define a class in multiple files. At compilation time, the files are merged together to compose the entire class definition. Using this approach, we are able to keep the pages (the XAML files) inside the specific platform's project while having the code behind files defined in the shared project. This way, we can have a common logic, applied to two different visual layouts.

The first step is to add a new code behind class in our shared project. It needs to have the same name of the XAML page we want to manage, plus the **.xaml.cs** extension. If, for example, we're working with a page called **MainPage.xaml,** we need to create in our shared a project a new class called **MainPage.xaml.cs**.

Then we need to define that it's a partial class, by simply adding the partial keyword to the class definition, like in the following sample:

```
namespace SampleApp
{
    public partial class MainPage
    {
    }
}
```

Now it's time to properly change the original code behind files, the ones that are defined in the platform's specific projects. Visual Studio doesn't allow us to delete a code behind file, so we just need to make sure that it contains only the class constructor, like in the following sample:

```
public sealed partial class MainPage : Page
{
    public MainPage()
    {
        this.InitializeComponent();
    }
}
```

Now we just need to add our logic in the code behind class defined in the shared project. It will automatically be merged with the original code behind classes during compilation, so that it will be automatically shared with both the Windows 8.1 and Windows Phone 8.1 applications.

The Model-View-ViewModel (MVVM) pattern

The Model-View-ViewModel (MVVM) pattern is the most-used approach when it comes to developing complex projects based on XAML technologies. When you develop an application using the traditional approach (based on logic included in the code behind files) it may become hard to keep a clear separation between the user interface and the logic. The code behind contains both code that interacts with the UI (for example, to trigger an animation or to apply a style) and code that performs business operations (like retrieving data from a web service or a database). This approach can make the code difficult to test and debug, especially if you're working in a team.

By using the MVVM pattern, you organize your code in three different components:

- The **Model**, which contains the entities and the repositories that define the data, that the application will manage. Typically, the model exposes raw data, which is independent from how they will be displayed in the application.
- The **View**, which is the user interface. In Universal Windows apps, Views are identified with the XAML pages.

- The **ViewModel** is the connection between the other components: it takes the raw data definitions from the Model and it elaborates them, so that they can be properly displayed in the View.

The MVVM pattern is based on some of the fundamental concepts we've previously learned in this chapter: the ViewModel is nothing but a standard class, which is set as `DataContext` of an entire XAML page. This way, thanks to the binding, you'll be able to connect all the properties defined in the ViewModel to the controls included in the page. The Windows Runtime also offers a special property called `Command`, which is a way to manage events (like the `Click` on a `Button` control) without using an event handler, and can be defined only in code behind. This way, you'll be able to react to the user's interaction directly in the ViewModel.

The MVVM pattern is particularly useful when you want to develop a Universal Windows app. Since there's a strict separation between logic and user interface, it's much easier to share the code (in our case, a ViewModel) with two different Views. The MVVM pattern is very powerful, but also complex to learn and master, especially in the beginning. Heavy use of binding can lead to potential performance issues, so it's important to learn how to use the MVVM pattern as a tool (which should be adapted to your need) rather than a fixed set of rules that you need to follow without questioning or changing them. Consequently, it won't be discussed in detail in this book. However, you can find a lot of tutorials and documentation about it, especially when it comes to the most popular available toolkits to implement it, which are MVVM Light (http://www.mvvmlight.net/), Caliburn Micro (https://github.com/Caliburn-Micro/) and Prism (https://prismwindowsruntime.codeplex.com/).

Conditional compilation

In the first chapter, we learned that Windows Phone 8.1 greatly improved the Windows Runtime convergence between Windows and Windows Phone. However, the full convergence goal has not been reached yet, so it may happen that, in your application, you need to use some code that works only in one of the two platforms.

The IntelliSense feature included in Visual Studio can help developers identify these scenarios, as you can see in the following image:

Figure 9: Visual Studio highlights that some properties are available only on Windows Phone.

In this sample, we're using a class called **ToastNotification**, which will be detailed in Chapter 10. For our purposes, it's enough to know that it's used to create and send toast notifications from the application. As you can see, the IntelliSense is notifying the developer that some properties (like **Group** or **SuppressPopup**) are available just in Windows Phone: these properties, in fact, are connected to the new Action Center, which is not available on Windows.

To properly manage these situations, Visual Studio offers a feature called **context switcher**, which is a dropdown menu placed on the top-left corner that can be used to change, at any time, the current context of the application: Windows or Windows Phone. IntelliSense will show you only the APIs and properties that are available in the selected context. For example, if you had chosen Windows as the current context, the properties we saw in the previous image (like **Group** or **SuppressPopup**) would have been hidden.

Figure 10: The context switcher in Visual Studio

Whie the context switcher is useful to determine which APIs are available on both platforms and which are not, it doesn't help to solve an important problem: what if we need to define some code in a shared class that is only able to run on one of the two platforms?

Please welcome **conditional compilation**: the philosophy behind it is the same of the traditional conditional programming, which allows you to execute a code block only if a specific condition is satisfied. Conditional compilation works in the same way, but in this case, the code isn't only not executed, but not compiled at all. This way, you'll be able to use, in a shared class, APIs and properties that are available only on one platform.

To manage this scenario, the Universal Windows app projects already define two compilation symbols that can be used together with conditional compilation to determine if the project is being built for Windows or Windows Phone. Windows uses the **WINDOWS_APP** keyword, while Windows Phone uses the **WINDOWS_PHONE_APP** keyword. These symbols are defined in the project's properties. To see them, right-click on one of the two projects, choose **Properties**, and look for a field called **Conditional compilation symbols** in the **Build** section.

Let's see an example using the conditional compilation, which uses the same **ToastNotification** class we've previously seen.

```
ToastNotification notification = new ToastNotification(template);
#if WINDOWS_PHONE_APP
notification.SuppressPopup = true;
#endif
```

The first line of code, which creates a new **ToastNotification** object, is normally executed, since it's available on both platforms. However, the **SuppressPopup** property is set only inside a conditional compilation block. The block is defined using the **#if** keyword, followed by the compilation symbol; once the conditional block is finished, you need to close it using the **#endif** keyword. In the previous sample, since the **SuppressPopup** property is available only on Windows Phone, we're using **WINDOWS_PHONE_APP** as compilation symbol.

Managing references in a Universal Windows app

In the first chapter of the book, you learned to use NuGet, which is a useful tool to easily add third-party libraries to your project. When it comes to Universal Windows apps, however, there's a point to highlight: the shared project isn't a real application, so you won't be able to add a reference directly to it. Consequently, if you need to use an external library in a class declared in the shared project, you'll need to add a reference to both specific projects, by using NuGet, or manually with the **Add reference** option offered by Visual Studio. As already mentioned in Chapter 1, a good way to deal with a Universal Windows app project is to right-click on the solution and choose the **Manage NuGet packages for Solution** option. Then, you can easily install a package in both projects.

Asynchronous programming

Asynchronous programming is one of the basic concepts when it comes to developing mobile applications. In the past, most applications were developed using a synchronous approach: until the running operation was completed, the application was basically frozen, and the user didn't have the chance to interact with it.

This approach doesn't play well with mobile applications: no one would buy a smartphone or a tablet that doesn't allow to the user to answer a call or to reply to mail until the current application has finished its task. The Windows Runtime offers two different ways to manage asynchronous programming: callbacks, and the async/await pattern.

Callbacks

If you have worked in the past with other development platforms, you have probably used the callbacks approach. In Windows Runtime, this approach is not widely used anymore, since most of the APIs rely on the async/await pattern. Still, there are some classes that are using this approach, especially when their purpose is to act as a listener to detect when something changes (for example, the geo localization services use the callback approach to track the user's movement).

Callbacks are delegate methods that are invoked when an asynchronous operation is ended or has detected a change compared to the previous value. With this approach, the code that starts the operation and the code that manages it is split into two different methods. Let's see some code, based on the example previously mentioned: the geo localization services, which are managed using the **Geolocator** class.

```
private void OnStartGeolocator(object sender, RoutedEventArgs e)
{
    Geolocator geolocator = new Geolocator();
    geolocator.PositionChanged += geolocator_PositionChanged;
    Debug.WriteLine("Finding the user's position...");
}

void geolocator_PositionChanged(Geolocator sender, PositionChangedEventArgs
args)
{
    Latitude.Text = args.Position.Coordinate.Latitude.ToString();
    Longitude.Text = args.Position.Coordinate.Longitude.ToString();
}
```

As you can see, we're using two different methods to properly track the user's position: the **OnStartGeolocator()** method takes care of initizialing the **GeoLocator** class and of subscribing to the **PositionChanged** event. The real tracking, instead, is made by the **geolocator_PositionChanged()** event handler, which is invoked every time the user's position changes.

Typically, the event handler used to manage the callback receives two parameters as input: the first one, **sender**, is the object that triggered the event; the second one contains some useful parameters to understand what's going on. In the previous sample, you can see that the second parameter's type is **PositionChangedEventArgs**, and it contains a **Position** property, with the coordinates of the user's position.

The code we've just written is asynchronous: the message in the Visual Studio's Output Windows (printed using the **Debug.Writeline()** method) is displayed immediately, right after the tracking has started. The callback's method is executed only when a new position is detected.

The async and await pattern

The callback approach makes the code harder to understand and manage for the developer: unlike synchronous code, the execution flow isn't linear, but it jumps from one method to another. The async and await pattern was introduced in C# 5.0 to solve this problem. The Windows Runtime heavily relies on this approach: it's used by every API that defines an operation that can require more than 50 ms to be completed.

When we use the async and await pattern we write sequential code, like it's synchronous: the compiler will execute one row at a time. Under the hood, the compiler will add a bookmark every time you'll start an asynchronous operation, and then will quit from the current method. This way, the UI thread will be released and the application will continue to be fast and responsive. Once the asynchronous operation is terminated, the compiler will resume the execution from the previously set bookmark.

The async and await pattern is heavily based on the **Task** class, which is the base type returned by every asynchronous operation. A method can return two different types:

- **Task**, in case it's a void method, that doesn't return any value to the caller, but simply performs some operations.
- **Task<T>**, in case the method returns a value to the caller. In this case, the compiler will wait until the operation is completed, and then it will return the result (which type is T) to the caller.

Let's see a real example, using the same **Geolocator** class we used to explain the callback approach. In this case, we won't subscribe to keep track of the user's movement, but we will ask for a single position, using a method called **GetGeopositionAsync()** (notice the **Async** suffix).

```
private async void OnGetPositionClicked(object sender, RoutedEventArgs e)
{
    Geolocator geolocator = new Geolocator();
    Geoposition geoposition = await geolocator.GetGeopositionAsync();
    Latitude.Text = geoposition.Coordinate.Latitude.ToString();
    Longitude.Text = geoposition.Coordinate.Longitude.ToString();
}
```

We can see the two key features required to properly use an asynchronous method. The first one is that the method definition needs to contain the **async** keyword. Then, we are able to add the **await** prefix before calling the asynchronous method (in our case, the **GetGeopositionAsync()**). Thanks to this keyword, the runtime will wait until the operation is completed before moving on. The result is that, until the geolocation services have returned the user's position, the application won't display the user's coordinates on the page.

As you can see, this code is much simpler to read and write, and it's completely asynchronous: the operation will be executed on a different thread than the one that manages the user interface, keeping the application fast and responsive.

It's important to highlight that, as a general rule, every asynchronous operation needs to return a **Task** or a **Task<T>** object. If you declare an asynchronous method that simply returns **void**, the behavior could be unpredictable. The only exception is when you're dealing with event handlers, like in the previous sample. Since they are "fire and forget" methods (you don't need to wait that, for example, the **Click** event on a **Button** is completed to execute the operation), you can mark them as **async void**.

The dispatcher

When you're working with asynchronous code, typically the code is executed on multiple threads, so the UI thread is free to keep the interface fast and responsive. However, it can happen that you need to interact with a page's control from a secondary thread. The problem is that, if you try to do it, the application will crash with the following exception:

The application called an interface that was marshalled for a different thread.
(Exception from HRESULT: 0x8001010E (RPC_E_WRONG_THREAD))

This issue happens because you can't interact with the user interface from a background thread. If you're using the async and await pattern, however, you won't have to deal with this problem: the pattern automatically takes care of returning the result from the secondary thread to the main one. In fact, as you can see in the previous sample, we didn't do anything special to display the user's position on the screen. We've simply retrieved the coordinates using the **GetGeopositionAsync()** method, and we've assigned the results to the **Text** property of a couple of **TextBlock** controls.

However, you don't always have the chance to use the async and await pattern. Let's consider the previous sample about using the callback approach.

```
private void OnStartGeolocator(object sender, RoutedEventArgs e)
{
    Geolocator geolocator = new Geolocator();
    geolocator.PositionChanged += geolocator_PositionChanged;
    Debug.WriteLine("Finding the user's position…");
}

void geolocator_PositionChanged(Geolocator sender, PositionChangedEventArgs args)
{
    Latitude.Text = args.Position.Coordinate.Latitude.ToString();
    Longitude.Text = args.Position.Coordinate.Longitude.ToString();
}
```

The previous code will generate an exception at runtime. The callback's method, in fact, is executed on a background thread, while the **TextBlock** controls we're trying to update are managed by the UI thread.

For these situations, the Windows Runtime offers a class called **Dispatcher**, which takes care of forwarding the operation to the UI thread. Here is the proper way to declare the previous sample:

```
private void OnStartGeolocator(object sender, RoutedEventArgs e)
{
    Geolocator geolocator = new Geolocator();
    geolocator.PositionChanged += geolocator_PositionChanged;
    Debug.WriteLine("Finding the user's position…");
}

void geolocator_PositionChanged(Geolocator sender, PositionChangedEventArgs args)
{
    Dispatcher.RunAsync(CoreDispatcherPriority.Normal, () =>
    {
        Latitude.Text = args.Position.Coordinate.Latitude.ToString();
        Longitude.Text = args.Position.Coordinate.Longitude.ToString();
    });
```

```
}
```

The operations that need to be executed on the UI thread (in our case, assigning the user's position to the `Text` property of a `TextBlock` control) are wrapped inside an anonymous method, which is passed as parameter of the `RunAsync()` method exposed by the `Dispatcher` class. The first parameter represents the priority of the operation: the suggested one is, usually, `Normal`. This way, the whole callback's method will be executed on a background thread, but the operations performed by the `RunAsync()` method will be executed on the UI thread. It's important to forward with the `Dispatcher` only the operations that really need to interact with the page. If, for example, we wanted to perform some additional operations to the user's position before displaying the coordinates on the page (like converting the coordinates in a civic address), we should perform them outside the dispatcher.

Chapter 3 Creating the User Interface: The Controls

The Windows Runtime offers a rich set of native controls that can be used to define the page's visual layout. When it comes to creating a Universal Windows app, we need to consider that we're developing an application that targets two different platforms that, despite the similarities, offer a different user experience, mostly due to the different form factors.

Consequently, in this chapter we'll see in detail three different control categories:

- **Common**: These controls offer the same visual layout and user experience both on Windows and on Windows Phone.
- **Optimized**: These controls have the same behavior on both platforms, but they offer a different visual experience, to better match the platform's one.
- **Signature**: This category includes all the controls that are available only on a specific platform.

Most of the controls described in this chapter belong to the Common category: otherwise, the proper category will be specified each time.

Layout controls

Layout controls are special controls that, most of the time, aren't visible on the page. Their purpose is to define the layout of the page, and they usually act as a container of other controls.

StackPanel

The `StackPanel` control can be used to place the nested controls one below the other, which will automatically adapt to fit all the available space.

Figure 11: The StackPanel control

You can also choose to align the nested controls horizontally, by setting the `Orientation` property to `Horizontal`, like in the following sample:

```
<StackPanel Orientation="Horizontal">
```

```
    <TextBlock Text="First Text" />
    <TextBlock Text="Second Text" />
</StackPanel>
```

Grid

The **Grid** control is used to create table layouts, where nested controls are organized in rows and columns. Here is a sample code:

```
<Grid>
    <Grid.RowDefinitions>
        <RowDefinition Height="50" />
        <RowDefinition MaxHeight="100" />
    </Grid.RowDefinitions>
    <Grid.ColumnDefinitions>
        <ColumnDefinition Width="200" />
        <ColumnDefinition Width="*" />
    </Grid.ColumnDefinitions>

    <TextBlock Text="Text placed in the first row of the second column"
Grid.Row="0" Grid.Column="1" />
</Grid>
```

The layout is defined using the **RowDefinitions** and **ColumnDefinitions** properties. Each of them can contain one or more **RowDefinition** or **ColumnDefinition** elements, according to the number of rows and columns you want to create. For every table element, you can specify a fixed height or width, or otherwise, use relative values, like "*" so that the row/column automatically adapts to its parent container, or "Auto", which adapts the row/column to its content. Relative values are very common when designing the user interface of a Windows Store application, since the layout can automatically adapt to the screen size and to the resolution of the device.

To define the cell where a control is placed, you need to use two special attached properties, called **Grid.Row** and **Grid.Column**, which can be added to any control. These properties simply contain the row and column number where the control is placed, starting from 0 as base index (so, if you've defined two columns, they will be identified by the indexes 0 and 1).

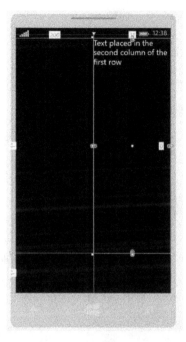

Figure 12: The Grid control

Canvas

The **Canvas** control leaves the maximum flexibility to the developer, since it uses a fixed placement. Using the attached properties **Canvas.Top** and **Canvas.Left**, that can be applied to any control, you can set the exact distance (in pixels) where the control should be placed, starting from the top left.

However, you need to be careful using this control: since it provides a fixed placement, it isn't able to automatically adapt the content to the screen's size and resolution, making it hard to create a layout that is pleasant to see both on a small tablet and on a big monitor.

```
<Canvas Width="640" Height="480" Background="White">
    <Rectangle Canvas.Left="30" Canvas.Top="30" Fill="Red" Width="200"
Height="200" />
</Canvas>
```

The previous samples shows a **Rectangle** control that is placed at the coordinates 30,30 starting from the top left.

VariableSizedWrapGrid

The **VariableSizedWrapGrid** control is able to automatically split the layout in multiple rows and columns: unlike in the **Grid** control, you won't have to manually specify the number of rows and columns to create, but you'll just have to set the maximum number of items to place in a row or in a column and its size.

Here's an example to help you understand how it works:

```
<VariableSizedWrapGrid MaximumRowsOrColumns="2" ItemHeight="200"
ItemWidth="200">
    <Rectangle Fill="Red" />
    <Rectangle Fill="Blue" />
    <Rectangle Fill="Orange" />
    <Rectangle Fill="Green" />
    <Rectangle Fill="Brown" />
</VariableSizedWrapGrid>
```

As you can see, we've set the size of a single item (using the **ItemHeight** and the **ItemWidth** properties) and the maximum number of rows and columns to create (using the **MaximumRowsOrColumns** property). Inside the **VariableSizedWrapGrid** control, we've placed five **Rectangle** controls. The result will be that, since we've set two as the maximum number of items, they will be automatically split in two rows.

Figure 13: A set of Rectangle controls placed inside a VariableSizedWrapGrid control

As default behavior, the nested items are split into rows: as you can see from Figure 13, the control has aligned the five rectangles into two rows. If you want to change this behavior and split items based on columns, you can set the **Orientation** property to **Horizontal**, like in the following sample:

```
<VariableSizedWrapGrid MaximumRowsOrColumns="2" ItemHeight="200"
```

```
ItemWidth="200" Orientation="Horizontal">
    <Rectangle Fill="Red" />
    <Rectangle Fill="Blue" />
    <Rectangle Fill="Orange" />
    <Rectangle Fill="Green" />
    <Rectangle Fill="Brown" />
</VariableSizedWrapGrid>
```

ScrollViewer

The **ScrollViewer** control acts as a container like the previous controls, but it doesn't try to arrange the layout of the nested controls. This means that it needs to be used in combination with other layout controls.

The **ScrollViewer** control is used when you need to display content that takes more space than the screen's size. The following sample shows how to manage a long text that doesn't fit the screen. Thanks to the **ScrollViewer** control, the user will be able to scroll the text down to keep reading it.

```
<ScrollViewer>
        <TextBlock TextWrapping="Wrap" Text="This can be a long text" />
</ScrollViewer>
```

Border

The **Border** control is able to wrap nested controls inside a border. By using the **BorderThickness** and **BorderBrush** properties, you can set the border's thickness and color. The following sample shows an **Image** control wrapped inside a red border, with a 5-pixel thickness:

```
<Border BorderThickness="5" BorderBrush="Red">
    <Image Source="/Assets/Image.jpg"/>
</Border>
```

As default behavior, the **BorderThickness** value is applied to every side of the border. However, you can also customize it by specifying a different thickness for each side (in the following order: left, top, right, bottom), like in the following sample.

```
<Border BorderThickness="10, 15, 20, 15" BorderBrush="Red">
    <Image Source="/Assets/Image.jpg"/>
</Border>
```

Figure 14: A Border control with different thickness for each side

Output controls

In this category, we'll see all the controls that are used to display information to the user, like texts, images, etc.

TextBlock

The **TextBlock** control is most widely used to display text in a page. The most important property is called **Text**, and contains the text that will be displayed. In addition, you can customize the text's look and feel, thanks to properties like **FontSize** (to change the dimension) and **FontStyle** (to change the font's type). Another property that is often used is called **TextWrapping**; when it's set to **Wrap**, it makes sure that the text is wrapped in multiple lines, in case it's too long.

```
<TextBlock Text="This is a long text" TextWrapping="Wrap" />
```

Another interesting property is called **TextTrimming**. When this feature is enabled, if the text is too long, it will be automatically trimmed and ellipses will be added at the end, so the user can understand that the text is cut off. You can apply two types of trimming: **CharacterEllipsis** (the text is cut at character level) or **WordEllipsis** (the text is cut at word level).

```
<TextBlock Text="This is a trimmed text" TextTrimming="CharacterEllipsis" />
```

You can also apply different styles to various parts of the text without having to split it in multiple **TextBlock** controls, thanks to the **Run** control. It's enough to add, inside a **TextBlock** control, one or more **Run** controls: each of them will contain a part of the text. You can also use the **LineBreak** control if you want to manually split the text into multiple lines.

```xml
<TextBlock>
    <Run Text="First line" />
    <LineBreak />
    <Run Text="Second line in bold" FontWeight="Bold" />
</TextBlock>
```

RichTextBlock

The **RichTextBlock** control is a more powerful version of **TextBlock**, since it offers more flexibility to the developer. You'll be able to create complex layouts by:

- Splitting the text in multiple paragraphs, using the **Paragraph** control.
- Changing the style of a text portion, using tags likes **Bold**, **Italic**, or **Underline**.
- Adding other XAML controls, using the **InlineUIContainer** control.

Let's see an example:

```xml
<RichTextBlock>
    <Paragraph>
        <Bold>This is a bold text</Bold>
    </Paragraph>
    <Paragraph>
        <Italic>This is an italic text</Italic>
    </Paragraph>
    <Paragraph>
        <Underline>This is an underlined text</Underline>
    </Paragraph>
    <Paragraph>
        <InlineUIContainer>
            <Image Source="/Assets/image.jpg" Width="200" />
        </InlineUIContainer>
    </Paragraph>
</RichTextBlock>
```

The **RichTextBlock** control contains multiple **Paragraph** controls, each one with some text that is formatted in different ways. In addition, we've used the **InlineUIContainer** control to display an image at the bottom of the text.

Figure 15: The RichTextBlocx control

Image

The **Image** control is used to display an image in the page. The image path is set using the **Source** property, which supports different kind of sources: the image can be stored on a remote address, in the application's package, or in the local storage. In Chapter 5, we'll see in detail the different ways we have to access to the various kind of storages using an URI address.

The following sample code shows an **Image** control that displays a remote image:

```
<Image Source="http://www.website.com/image.png" />
```

The **Image** control offers also built-in support to the crop feature, so that you can easily display a smaller part of the image. This feature is implemented using the **Clip** property, which accepts a **RectangleGeometry** control, which defines the crop area, like in the following sample:

```
<Image Source="http://www.website.com/image.png">
    <Image.Clip>
        <RectangleGeometry Rect="0, 0, 100, 100" />
    </Image.Clip>
</Image>
```

The crop is defined with four values: the first two identify the X and Y coordinate of the area's starting point (0, 0 represents the top-left corner of the image), while the other two represent the size of the crop area (in the sample, the rectangle's size is 100 x 100).

Another important property is **Stretch**, which is used to define how the image will fill the available space:

- **Uniform** (the default value): The image is resized to fit the control's size by keeping the original ratio, so that it doesn't look distorted.
- **Fill**: The image is stretched to use all the available space, even if it means ignoring the ratio and creating a distorted effect when the control has a different size.
- **UniformToFill**: It's a combination of the previous modes. The image is automatically cropped to create a new image that keeps the same ratio of the original one, and at the same time, fills all the available space.
- **None**: The image is displayed using the original size, regardless of the size of the control.

Input controls

In this category, we'll take a look at the main controls that are used to receive input from the user.

TextBox and PasswordBox

The **TextBox** control is the simplest one for getting text input from the user: it works like the **TextBlock** control, except that the **Text** property isn't used only to set the text to display, but also to grab the text inserted by the user.

A useful property offered by the control is called **PlaceholderText**, which defines a placeholder text that can be displayed inside the box as a hint for the user, so that she can better understand which kind of input we're expecting. As soon as the user starts to type into the box, the placeholder text will disappear.

Another important scenario to keep in mind is that Windows Store apps are usually used with a touch interface. Instead of a real keyboard, the user will insert the text using a virtual keyboard. As developers, we have the chance to customize the virtual keyboard so that it's optimized for the kind of input we're asking for the user. This customization is achieved using the **InputScope** property, which can assume many values like:

- **Url** to display a keyboard optimized to enter web addresses.
- **Number** to display a keyboard optimized to enter numbers.
- **EmailSmtpAddress** to display a keyboard optimized to enter a mail address.

We can also enable or disable the auto correction feature (using the **IsSpellCheckEnabled** property) or the text prediction feature, which suggests words to the user while he's typing on the keyboard (using the **IsTextPredictionEnabled** property).

Here is a sample code to define a **TextBox** control:

```
<TextBox IsSpellCheckEnabled="True" IsTextPredictionEnabled="True"
```

```
PlaceholderText="Placeholder Text" Text="Input text" />
```

The Windows Runtime also offers a custom **TextBox** control called **PasswordBox**. It works exactly like a **TextBox** but, by default, it replaces the inserted text with dots so that the user's input isn't visible on the screen. As you can imagine, it's perfect for scenarios where we're asking for sensitive data, like passwords or credit card numbers. Since the text is automatically hidden, the **PasswordBox** control doesn't offer many ways to customize it as the **TextBox** control. The only important available option is called **IsPasswordRevealButtonEnabled**; when it's set to **True**, it adds a button at the end of the box that, when pressed, temporarily displays the text, so that the user can see if he inserted the correct password.

DatePicker and TimePicker

The **DatePicker** and **TimePicker** controls are used to manage date and times in an application. These controls are part of the optimized category: they work towards the same result on both platforms, but they have a different visual layout. In Windows, they are displayed as a series of dropdown menus, while in Windows Phone, they will trigger the navigation to a new page, with sets of boxes, one for each part of the date or time.

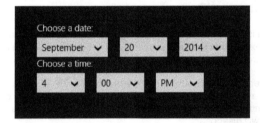

Figure 16: The DatePicker and TimePicker controls in Windows 8.1

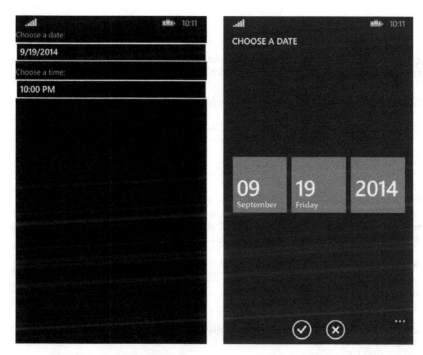

Figure 17: The DatePicker and TimePicker controls in Windows Phone 8.1

As default behavior, the **DatePicker** control displays all the date fields, which are the day, the month, and the year. It's possible to hide them by using the properties called **YearVisible**, **MonthVisible**, or **DayVisible**. If one or more fields is hidden, the control will automatically return to the application the current value (so, for example, if you hide the year, the control will return the current year).

```
<DatePicker x:Name="Date" YearVisible="False" />
```

You can also define the date range by using the **MinYear** and **MaxYear** properties, which can be useful for many scenarios, like asking the user's birthday. In this case, it would be useless to display years prior to 1900 or later than the current year. However, these properties can't be set in XAML, but only in code behind, since their type is **DateTimeOffset**, which can't be expressed in XAML.

```
protected override void OnNavigatedTo(NavigationEventArgs e)
{
    DateTime minYear = new DateTime(1900, 1, 1);
    Date.MinYear = new DateTimeOffset(minYear);
    Date.MaxYear = new DateTimeOffset(DateTime.Now);
```

```
}
```

If you want to retrieve, in the code behind, the date selected by the user, you need to use the **Date** property, like in the following sample, which shows the date using a pop-up message:

```
private async void OnGetDateClicked(object sender, RoutedEventArgs e)
{
    DateTimeOffset selectedDate = Birthday.Date;
    MessageDialog dialog = new MessageDialog(selectedDate.ToString());
    await dialog.ShowAsync();
}
```

The **TimePicker** control works in a similar way, but unlike the **DatePicker** control, it's composed of only two elements: hour and minute. You can customize the time range using the **MinuteIncrement** property so that instead of displaying all the possible values for the minute field (from 0 to 59), it will show only the specified range.

Let's see, for example, the following implementation:

```
<TimePicker MinuteIncrement="15" />
```

By using the previous XAML code, the minute dropdown list will display just the values 00, 15, 30, and 45, instead of all the values from 0 to 59.

The value selected by the user in the **TimePicker** control is stored in the **Time** property using a **TimeSpan** object. The following sample shows a method that displays the selected time converted into hours to the user using a pop-up message:

```
private async void OnGetDateClicked(object sender, RoutedEventArgs e)
{
    TimeSpan timeSpan = StartTime.Time;
    MessageDialog dialog = new MessageDialog(timeSpan.TotalHours.ToString());
    await dialog.ShowAsync();
}
```

Both controls also support setting a header, which is displayed above the control, with the **Header** property.

Button and ToggleButton

The **Button** control is the simplest available control for interacting with a user: when it's pressed, it raises the **Click** event, which you can manage in code behind. The button's content is defined by the **Content** property, which can contain a simple text, like in the following sample:

```
<Button Content="Click me" Click="OnButtonClicked" />
```

The **Content** property can also be expressed with the extended syntax: in this case, you can use any XAML control to define the button's layout. The following sample shows how to define a **Button** control using an image:

```
<Button Click="OnButtonClicked">
    <Button.Content>
        <Image Source="image.png" />
    </Button.Content>
</Button>
```

The Windows Runtime also introduced a new kind of button control, called **ToggleButton**. It works and behave like a regular button, but it's also able to manage two different kind of states: enabled and disabled. Consequently, the control offers also a property called **IsChecked**, which type is **Boolean**: when the button is enabled, its value is **true**; otherwise, the value is **false**.

The following sample code shows a simple usage of the control:

```
<ToggleButton Content="This is a ToggleButton" IsChecked="True" />
```

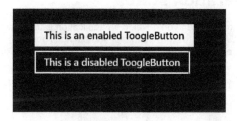

Figure 18: The two different states that a ToggleButton control can assume

RadioButton and CheckBox

The **RadioButton** and **CheckBox** controls are both used to give multiple choices to the user. They share many features, like:

- The text displayed near the control is set using the **Content** property.
- To check if the control has been selected, you need to use the **IsChecked** property.
- If you want to intercept when the user taps on the control, you can use the **Checked** and **Unchecked** events.

The biggest difference between the **RadioButton** and **CheckBox** controls is that the **RadioButton** can be defined as part of a group. In this case, the user will be able to enable only one of them. If they try to enable another one, the previously enabled control will be automatically deactivated. With the **CheckBox** control, instead, the user can enable as many of the options as they prefer.

The **RadioButton**'s grouping is achieved using the **Group** property: by assign to a set of **RadioButton** controls the same value, the user will be able to enable just one of them at a time. Here is a sample on how to use both controls:

```xml
<StackPanel>
    <CheckBox Content="First option" />
    <CheckBox Content="Second option" />
    <CheckBox Content="Third option" />

    <RadioButton Content="First option" GroupName="Options" />
    <RadioButton Content="Second option" GroupName="Options" />
    <RadioButton Content="Third option" GroupName="Options" />
</StackPanel>
```

Show the operation status

A very common requirement when you develop an application is to show to the user status of an operation in progress. We need to warn them that something is going on and, until the operation is finished, the application may not be fully ready to use. The Windows Runtime includes two controls to achieve this goal.

ProgressRing

The **ProgressRing** control is used for loading operations that are preventing the user from interacting with the application. Until the operation is finished, there isn't anything else for the user to do, so he just needs to wait (for example, a news reader is loading the latest news and, until the operation is completed, the user doesn't have any content to interact with). The control simply displays a spinning ring, which will notify to the user that an operation is in progress.

Using this control is very simple: the animation is controlled by the **IsActive** property, which type is **Boolean**. When its value is **true**, the progress ring will spin; when it's **false**, instead, the progress ring will be hidden. Typically, you're going to show it before the operation starts; then, you'll hide it once the job is finished. Here is a sample XAML declaration of this control:

```xml
<ProgressRing x:Name="Progress" />
```

Here is, instead, how you ideally manage a loading operation in code (for example, downloading some data from Internet) using a **ProgressRing** control:

```
protected override void OnNavigatedTo(NavigationEventArgs e)
{
    Progress.IsActive = true;
    //start loading the data
    Progress.IsActive = false;
}
```

ProgressBar

The **ProgressBar** control, unlike the **ProgressRing** control, can be used in scenarios where the operation happens in the background and the user is able to keep interacting with the application even while the operation is in progress. The **ProgressBar** control is rendered with a bar that is filled using the **Value** property: you can assign a numeric value from 0 (empty bar) to 100 (full bar). This feature makes the control useful also for operations where you can exactly determine its status, like downloading a file from Internet.

For example, during a download operation, you can determine how many bytes have been downloaded of the total size file and calculate the percentage to set in the **Value** property. This way, the user can be continuously updated on the download status.

The **ProgressBar** control can also be used to notify the user that an operation is in progress, without displaying the exact status: by setting the **IsIndeterminate** property to **true**, in fact, the bar will be replaced by a series of dots, that will continuously move from the left to the right of the screen.

```
<ProgressRing x:Name="Progress" IsIndeterminate="True" />
```

Displaying collections of data

One of the most common requirements in mobile applications is to display a collection of data: we've already seen in Chapter 2 how this scenario can be easily implemented using binding and data templates. In this section, we'll see the most important controls available in the Windows Runtime to display collections.

GridView and ListView

GridView and ListView are the two controls most frequently used to display data collections in the Windows Store app, since they're able to provide a look and feel that is consistent with the platform's guidelines. Both controls offer the same features and properties; the main difference is that the GridView control can be scrolled through horizontally, using a grid structure, while the ListView control is rendered using a traditional list that the user can scroll from the top to the bottom.

Showing flat collections

The simplest way to use these controls is to display flat data collections. In this case, they behave like every other standard control to display lists, which means:

- You need to define a DataTemplate for the ItemTemplate property, which defines the layout that is used to render each element of the collection.
- You need to assign the data collection you want to display to the ItemsSource property.

You need to manage the item selected by the user, using one of the approaches that will be detailed later. The following XAML code shows a sample definition of a flat collection displayed with a ListView control:

```
<ListView x:Name="List" SelectionChanged="List_OnSelectionChanged">
    <ListView.ItemTemplate>
        <DataTemplate>
            <StackPanel>
                <TextBlock Text="{Binding Path=Name}" />
                <TextBlock Text="{Binding Path=Surname}" />
            </StackPanel>
        </DataTemplate>
    </ListView.ItemTemplate>
</ListView>
```

The ItemTemplate of this list is configured to display a collection of objects with two properties called Name and Surname. Here is a sample definition of this object:

```
public class Person
{
    public string Name { get; set; }
    public string Surname { get; set; }
}
```

And here is how, in the code behind, we create a sample collection of Person objects and assign it to the ListView control:

```
protected override void OnNavigatedTo(NavigationEventArgs e)
{
```

```
List<Person> people = new List<Person>
{
    new Person
    {
        Name = "Matteo",
        Surname = "Pagani"
    },
    new Person
    {
        Name = "Angela",
        Surname = "Olivieri"
    }
};

List.ItemsSource = people;
}
```

Showing grouped collections

The most interesting feature offered by the ListView and GridView controls is grouped collections support: you'll be able to display a collection of data that is grouped in different categories. The user will be able to not only scroll through the list, but also to quickly jump from one category to another.

Both Windows and Windows Phone offer many examples of this approach. For example, if you open the People application, you will notice that contacts are grouped in different categories, according to the initial letter of the name. By tapping on a letter, a new view that displays all the available letters is opened, so that the user can quickly jump from one group of contacts to another.

Let's see a real example, by changing a bit the Person class we've previously defined:

```
public class Person
{
    public string Name { get; set; }
    public string Surname { get; set; }
    public string City { get; set; }
}
```

We've added a new property called City; we'll use it to group our collection of people by the city where they live in.

To achieve our goal, we need to introduce a new class offered by the Windows Runtime, called CollectionViewSource, which acts as a proxy between the data collection and the control that will display it (in our case, a GridView or a ListView control). Instead of connecting the ItemsSource property of the control directly to our collection, we'll connect it to this proxy class, which offers many advanced features, like automatic grouping support.

The **CollectionViewSource** can be defined in XAML as a regular resource. The following sample shows a **CollectionViewSource** object defined as page resource:

```
<Page.Resources>
    <CollectionViewSource x:Name="People" IsSourceGrouped="True" />
</Page.Resources>
```

As you can see, thanks to the **IsSourceGrouped** property, we've been able to easily specify that the data stored in this collection will be grouped. The next step is to connect our data to this proxy class. The procedure is similar to the one we've seen for a flat list, except that this time we need to specify the group criteria. We can easily do it thanks to LINQ and to the **GroupBy()** extension. Here is an example:

```
protected override void OnNavigatedTo(NavigationEventArgs e)
{
    List<Person> people = new List<Person>
    {
        new Person
        {
            Name = "Matteo",
            Surname = "Pagani",
            City = "Como"
        },
        new Person
        {
            Name = "Ugo",
            Surname = "Lattanzi",
            City = "Milan"
        },
        new Person
        {
            Name = "Roberto",
            Surname = "Freato",
            City = "Milan"
        },
        new Person
        {
            Name = "Massimo",
            Surname = "Bonanni",
            City = "Rome"
        }
    };
    var groups = people.GroupBy(x => x.City);
    People.Source = groups;
}
```

We've grouped the collection by the property called `City`, by applying the `GroupBy()` extension method on the original collection. Then, we've assigned the resulting grouped collection to the `Source` property of the `CollectionViewSource` object we've previously defined as resource in the page.

We're done working on the code, but our goal is not achieved yet, since we need to define the visual layout of the collection. By default, in fact, the `GridView` or the `ListView` control doesn't know how to visually display the groups: the `ItemTemplate` property just defines what a single item will look like, but not how the entire group will be rendered. Consequently, we need to apply some changes to the XAML definition of the control.

The following sample shows a `GridView` control configured to display our grouped collection:

```
<GridView ItemsSource="{Binding Source={StaticResource People}}">
    <GridView.ItemTemplate>
        <DataTemplate>
            <StackPanel>
                <TextBlock Text="{Binding Path=Name}" />
                <TextBlock Text="{Binding Path=Surname}" />
            </StackPanel>
        </DataTemplate>
    </GridView.ItemTemplate>
    <GridView.GroupStyle>
        <GroupStyle HidesIfEmpty="True">
            <GroupStyle.HeaderTemplate>
                <DataTemplate>
                    <Border Background="LightGray">
                        <TextBlock Text="{Binding Key}" Foreground="Black"
Margin="10" Style="{StaticResource HeaderTextBlockStyle}"/>
                    </Border>
                </DataTemplate>
            </GroupStyle.HeaderTemplate>
        </GroupStyle>
    </GridView.GroupStyle>
</GridView>
```

The first thing you'll notices is that we're setting the `ItemsSource` property in a different way: since the `CollectionViewSource` object has been defined as a resource, we assign it using the `StaticResource` markup extension.

Then we need to set up the different visual styles of the list:

- The first one shouldn't be a surprise: as we have done to manage a flat list, we define the `ItemTemplate`, which is the template used to render every single item of the collection. We're using the same one we've previously seen, which displays the name and the surname of the person.
- The second one is the `GroupStyle` element, which defines the behavior of the group. By setting the `HidesIfEmpty` property to `True`, we make sure that a group isn't displayed if there are no elements in it.

- The **GroupStyle** control offers an important property called **HeaderTemplate**: it's the template used to render the group header, which is displayed at the beginning of each group. This goal is achieved by adding a **TextBlock** control, which is connected to the **Key** field. When we've grouped the collection using the **GroupBy()** method, we've basically created another collection with one element for each group (the user's city). Each element contains the list of items that belong to the group (the people that live in that city), and has a key (the **Key** property) with the name of the group. With this **DataTemplate**, we'll simply display a text with the name of the city, followed the list of people that live there.

The following image shows how the previous code is rendered in a real application.

Figure 19: A GridView control displays a grouped collection

As mentioned previously, the **ListView** control works in exactly the same way: by simply changing the previous code by replacing all the references to the **GridView** control, we will be able to turn the grid into a traditional vertical list, like in the following image:

Figure 20: The same collection displayed using a ListView control

Managing the item selection

The most common requirement when you work with a collection of data is to manage the selection: the user taps on one of the items, and we want to detect which has been selected so that we can perform additional operations (like redirecting the user to a detail page). There are four ways to manage selection; you can choose your favorite one by setting the **SelectionMode** property:

- **Single** (the default): The user can select only one item, which is highlighted until another item is selected.
- **Multiple**: This mode allows the user to select multiple items. Every time she taps on an item, it's automatically added to the list of selected items.
- **Extended**: It's a combination of the previous two modes. The single tap triggers a standard selection, while a right-click with the mouse or a swipe on the item towards the bottom of the screen will add it to the list of selected items.
- **None**: This mode disables the selection. No items can be selected, and the **SelectionChanged** event is not triggered.

Except for **None**, every other mode always triggers the **SelectionChanged** event when the user taps on one item. The only difference is that, in case of single selection, we can use just the **SelectedItem** property of the control, which contains the selected item. Otherwise, in case of multiple selection, we can use the **SelectedItems** property, which is a collection that contains all the flagged items.

The following sample shows how to use the **SelectedItem** property when the
SelectionChanged event is triggered to display the name of the selected person with a pop-up:

```
private async void List_OnSelectionChanged(object sender,
SelectionChangedEventArgs e)
{
    Person selectedPerson = List.SelectedItem as Person;
    if (selectedPerson != null)
    {
        MessageDialog dialog = new MessageDialog(selectedPerson.Name);
        await dialog.ShowAsync();
    }
}
```

It's important to highlight that, since the **GridView** or **ListView** controls can display any
collection of data, the **SelectedItem** property is a generic **object**. Before accessing to its
properties, we need to cast it to the type we're expecting (in our case, it's a collection of **Person**
objects).

The following sample, instead, shows a similar scenario, but with multiple selections enabled. In
this case, we display to the user the number of items he selected in the list.

```
private async void List_OnSelectionChanged(object sender,
SelectionChangedEventArgs e)
{
    int selectedItems = List.SelectedItems.Count;
    MessageDialog dialog = new MessageDialog(selectedItems.ToString());
    await dialog.ShowAsync();
}
```

The **GridView** and **ListView** controls also offer an alternative way to manage the selection,
which is really useful when we don't perform any particular operation on the selected item, but
we just want, for example, to redirect the user to another page when the item is clicked. In this
mode, the items are treated like buttons: when you tap on one of them, an event called
ItemClick will be triggered, and it will contain, as parameter, the item that has been selected.

To enable this mode, you'll have to set the **IsItemClickEnabled** property to **True** and then
subscribe to the **ItemClick** event. Usually, when you enable this mode, it's also useful to set
the **SelectionMode** to **None**, to avoid overlapping the two selection modes and having both the
ItemClick and the **SelectionChanged** events triggered.

Managing the **ItemClick** event in the code behind is really easy, as you can see in the
following sample:

```
private async void List_OnItemClick(object sender, ItemClickEventArgs e)
{
    Person person = e.ClickedItem as Person;
```

```
    if (person != null)
    {
        MessageDialog dialog = new MessageDialog(person.Name);
        await dialog.ShowAsync();
    }
}
```

The event handler's parameter (which type is **ItemClickEventArgs**) contains a property called **ClickedItem**, with a reference to the selected item. As usual, since the control can display any type of data, the **ClickedItem** property contains a generic object, so we need to perform a cast before using it.

Semantic Zoom

Semantic Zoom is a feature that is part of the native experience offered by Windows and Windows Phone that offers the user a way to browse a collection of data in two different ways: a traditional view, with all the details (like the one we've just seen talking about the **GridView** and **ListView** controls), and an overview, which gives a quick glance of all the available groups, allowing the user to quickly jump from one to another.

Semantic Zoom is implemented in the same way on both platforms, but it's activated in a different way: on Windows 8.1 it's typically triggered by zooming out with two fingers on the touch screen or by clicking the "-" symbol displayed at the bottom right, while on Windows Phone 8.1, it's usually activated by tapping on one of the group's headers in the list.

To implement Semantic Zoom, the Windows Runtime offers a control called **SemanticZoom**, which is easy to understand:

```
<SemanticZoom>
    <SemanticZoom.ZoomedInView>
        <!-- standard visualization -->
    </SemanticZoom.ZoomedInView>
    <SemanticZoom.ZoomedOutView>
        <!-- groups visualization -->
    </SemanticZoom.ZoomedOutView>
</SemanticZoom>
```

The **SemanticZoom** control is able to manage two different statuses, represented by two specific properties: **ZoomedInView** defines the layout that displays the traditional list, with all the details. **ZoomedOutView**, instead, defines the layout that displays all the groups. Inside these properties, you can't define any arbitrary XAML: only controls that support the **ISemanticZoomInformation** interface are able to properly work with this feature. The Windows Runtime offers three native controls that support this interface: **GridView**, **ListView**, and **Hub**.

When it comes to managing the `ZoomedInView`, there's no difference compared to what we've learned about the `GridView` or the `ListView` controls. In this view, we need to manage the traditional list, so we're going to create a collection of data, define it as a `CollectionViewSource` object, and connect it to `ItemsSource` property of the control. The `ZoomedInView` property will contain a block of XAML code similar to the following one:

```
<Page.Resources>
    <CollectionViewSource x:Name="People" IsSourceGrouped="True" />
</Page.Resources>

<SemanticZoom>
    <SemanticZoom.ZoomedInView>
        <GridView ItemsSource="{Binding Source={StaticResource People}}">
            ...
        </GridView>
    </SemanticZoom.ZoomedInView>
</SemanticZoom>
```

As you can see, the `GridView` control is simply connected to the `CollectionViewSource` object, which has been defined as a page resource.

The `ZoomedOutView`, however, needs to be managed in a different way: when it's enabled, in fact, we don't need to display all the items in the collection, but just the groups the data is divided into. To achieve our goal, the `CollectionViewSource` offers a property called `CollectionGroups`, which contains all the groups the data is split into. Do you remember the sample we saw before with a list of people grouped by city? In our case, the `CollectionGroups` property will contain just the list of cities.

Here is a sample definition of the `ZoomedOutView` property:

```
<SemanticZoom>
    <SemanticZoom.ZoomedOutView>
        <GridView ItemsSource="{Binding Source={StaticResource People},
Path=CollectionGroups}">
            ...
        </GridView>
    </SemanticZoom.ZoomedOutView>
</SemanticZoom>
```

We're using, again, a `GridView` control to display the list of groups, but instead of binding the `ItemsSource` property directly with the `CollectionViewSource` object, we bind it to the specific `CollectionGroups` property.

The last step is to define the visual layout of the `ZoomedOutView` mode. We're using a standard `GridView` control, so we simply need to define the `ItemTemplate` property with a proper `DataTemplate`, like in the following sample:

```
<SemanticZoom>
    <SemanticZoom.ZoomedOutView>
        <GridView ItemsSource="{Binding Source={StaticResource
People},Path=CollectionGroups}">
            <GridView.ItemTemplate>
                <DataTemplate>
                    <Border Background="LightGray" Width="300" Padding="5">
                        <TextBlock Text="{Binding Group.Key}"
Foreground="Black" TextAlignment="Center" Style="{StaticResource
HeaderTextBlockStyle}" />
                    </Border>
                </DataTemplate>
            </GridView.ItemTemplate>
        </GridView>
    </SemanticZoom.ZoomedOutView>
    <SemanticZoom.ZoomedInView>
        <GridView ItemsSource="{Binding Source={StaticResource People}}">
            ...
        </GridView>
    </SemanticZoom.ZoomedInView>
</SemanticZoom>
```

It's a standard **DataTemplate**; the only thing to highlight is that the **TextBlock** control is connected to a property called **Group.Key**, which contains the name of the group that we want to display (in our case, the city).

The following image shows what happens in a Windows 8.1 application when you zoom out from the standard list:

Figure 21: The group list displayed using the SemanticZoom control

FlipView

The **FlipView** control offers another way to display a collection of items that is useful when you want to focus the user's attention on the selected item, like in a photo gallery. In fact, when you use the **FlipView** control, only the selected item is visible, and it occupies all the available space. The user needs to swipe to the left or to the right (or use the buttons that only Windows displays on both sides) to display the other items in the collection.

Except for this difference, the **FlipView** control behaves like a **GridView** or **ListView** control:

- You need to set the **ItemTemplate** property to define the layout of the selected item.
- You need to assign the collection of items to the **ItemsSource** property.
- You can subscribe to the **SelectionChanged** event to be notified every time the user swipes to the left or to the right to display another item.
- If you need to discover which item is currently displayed, you can use the **SelectedItem** property.

The following XAML code shows a sample definition of a **FlipView** control used to display an images gallery:

```
<FlipView x:Name="Images">
    <FlipView.ItemTemplate>
        <DataTemplate>
            <Grid>
                <Image Source="{Binding Image}" Stretch="UniformToFill"/>
                <Border Background="#A5000000" Height="80"
VerticalAlignment="Bottom">
                    <TextBlock Text="{Binding Title}" FontFamily="Segoe UI"
FontSize="26" Foreground="#CCFFFFFF" Padding="15,20"/>
                </Border>
            </Grid>
        </DataTemplate>
    </FlipView.ItemTemplate>
</FlipView>
```

Hub

The **Hub** control is one of the most important controls available in the Windows Runtime, since it's often used to define the main page of an application. The **Hub** control is composed of different sections, which are placed one next to the other: the user can swipe to the left or to the right of the screen to see the previous or the next section. To help users understand the sections concept, a section doesn't take the whole space on the page; the right margin is used to display a glimpse of the next section, so that the user can understand that there's more content to see and discover.

Typically, the **Hub** control isn't used to contain huge amounts of data, but to provide subsets of them, and to give quick access to the different sections of the applications. For example, in a news reader application, you won't use the **Hub** control to display all the available news; this duty can be assigned to a specific page of the application. However, a section of the **Hub** control could display just the most recent news, and then provide a link to see all of them.

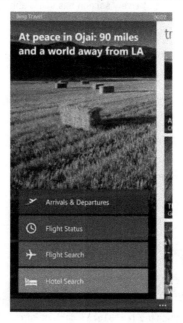

Figure 22: The Hub control used in a Windows Store application for Windows Phone

Here is a sample **Hub** control's definition:

```
<Hub Header="Page title">
    <HubSection Header="First section">
        <DataTemplate>
            <Image Source="/Assets/image.png" />
        </DataTemplate>
    </HubSection>
    <HubSection Header="Second section">
        <DataTemplate>
            <StackPanel>
                <TextBlock Text="Some content" />
            </StackPanel>
        </DataTemplate>
    </HubSection>
</Hub>
```

The **Hub** control can include a title, which is displayed at the top; it's set using the **Header** property, which accepts a simple string. You can also fully customize the header by defining a new template with the **HeaderTemplate** property.

As we've previously mentioned, the **Hub** control is split into different sections; each of them is identified by the **HubSection** control. Every section has some unique features:

- The **HubSection** control offers a property called **Header**, which contains the section's title, and is displayed at the top of every section.
- The content of the section is defined using a **DataTemplate**. It's important to highlight that, despite this behavior, the **Hub** control isn't able to display a collection of data; you can see, in fact, that the **ItemsSource** property is missing.

The choice of using a **DataTemplate** to define the section's look and feel has some challenges, compared to defining the layout of a simple page. In fact, since it's a **DataTemplate**, we can't simply assign a name to a control using the **x:Name** property and then access it in the code behind. The controls aren't part of the page, but are included in the **DataTemplate** connected to the **HubSection**.

Let's see a real example to better understand the issue. Take the following XAML code:

```
<Hub>
    <HubSection Header="First section">
        <DataTemplate>
            <TextBlock x:Name="Name" />
        </DataTemplate>
    </HubSection>
</Hub>
```

Normally, if you wanted to update the **TextBlock**'s content from code, you would have written an event handler similar to the following one:

```
private void OnButtonClicked(object sender, RoutedEventArgs e)
{
    Name.Text = "Matteo";
}
```

However, this code won't compile, since the **TextBlock** control identified by the keyword **Name** is defined inside a **DataTemplate**, and it can't be directly accessed. The solution is to use binding, as we learned about in Chapter 2.

The previous **Hub** control definition needs to be changed in the following way:

```
<Hub x:Name="MainHub">
    <HubSection Header="First section">
        <DataTemplate>
            <TextBlock Text="{Binding Name}" />
```

```
            </DataTemplate>
        </HubSection>
    </Hub>
```

We need also to change the code in the code behind to properly set the control's **DataContext**, so that it can find a property called **Name** to resolve the binding expression:

```
public MainPageView()
{
    this.InitializeComponent();
    Person person = new Person();
    person.Name = "Matteo";
    MainHub.DataContext = person;
}
```

Another feature supported by the **Hub** control is interactive headers: when we enable it, the user is able to tap on a **HubSection**'s header, so that we can perform additional operations or navigations. For example, a section could display only a couple of news items, but by tapping on the header, the user could be redirected to another page of the application where she can read all the available news.

To enable this feature, you'll need to set the **IsHeaderInteractive** property to **true** on every **HubSection** control you want to manage this way; then, you need to subscribe to the **SectionHeaderClick** that is offered directly by the **Hub** control.

The following sample shows a **Hub** control where the first section has been configured to support interactive headers:

```
<Hub SectionHeaderClick="Hub_OnSectionHeaderClick">
    <HubSection Header="First section" IsHeaderInteractive="True">
        <DataTemplate>
            <Image Source="/Assets/image.jpg" />
        </DataTemplate>
    </HubSection>
    <HubSection Header="Second section">
        <DataTemplate>
            <StackPanel>
                <TextBlock Text="Some content" />
            </StackPanel>
        </DataTemplate>
    </HubSection>
</Hub>
```

The following code shows how to manage the **SectionHeaderClick** event, so that we can be notified every time the user taps on a header:

```
private async void Hub_OnSectionHeaderClick(object sender,
HubSectionHeaderClickEventArgs e)
{
    MessageDialog dialog = new MessageDialog(e.Section.Header.ToString());
    await dialog.ShowAsync();
}
```

The event handler offers a parameter (which type is **HubSectionHeaderClickEventArgs**), which contains a property called **Header** that is the **HubSection** control that triggered the event. You can use it to understand which section has been tapped and perform the proper navigation. In the previous sample, we just display with a pop-up message the header of the selected section.

Pivot (Windows Phone only)

The **Pivot** control is a signature control, since it's available only on Windows Phone. The user experience is similar to the one offered by the tab controls in other platforms; the **Pivot** is split into different sections that the user can see by swiping to the left or to the right of the screen. In this case, however, every section will fit the entire size of the page. To help the user understand that there are other sections, a top bar will display the name of the other sections, with the current one highlighted with a different color.

The **Pivot** control is typically used in two scenarios:

- You need to show to the user the same information, but referred to different contexts. The Mail application is a good example: all the pivot's sections display the same information (emails), but filtered by different parameters (like unread, higher priority, etc.).
- You need to show to the user different information, but related to the same context. The People application is a good example: when you tap on a contact, you can see all the details, like phone number, photos posted on social networks, the latest interactions, etc. All of these information are stored in different sections of the page.

Figure 23: The Pivot control used in the Windows Phone's People application

The following sample shows how to use the **Pivot** control in an XAML page:

```
<Pivot Title="Page title">
    <PivotItem Header="First header">
        <StackPanel>
            <TextBlock Text="Some content" />
        </StackPanel>
    </PivotItem>
    <PivotItem Header="Second section">
        <StackPanel>
            <TextBlock Text="Some other content" />
        </StackPanel>
    </PivotItem>
</Pivot>
```

The `Pivot` control has a property called `Title`, which defines the title of the page. Every section, instead, is identified by a `PivotItem` control, which is nested inside the main `Pivot` control. Each can have its own title, which is the header displayed in the top bar; the property to set is called `Header`.

Except for these features, the `PivotItem` control acts as a simple container: you can place inside it any other XAML control you want, which will be rendered in the page when the current section is active.

The `Pivot` control can also be used to create guided procedures (like a configuration wizard). It offers a property called `IsLocked` that, when it's set to `true`, prevents the user from moving to another section. This way, for example, you can unlock the next section only when the user has filled all the required fields in the current section.

Managing the application bar: CommandBar and AppBar

The application bar concept is widely used by Windows and Windows Phone applications. It's a bar, usually hidden on Windows 8.1, that offers some specific functions to interact with the current context, or to navigate through the application.

An application bar can be placed in two different positions, which are identified by two properties offered by the `Page` class:

- `BottomAppBar` is used to define the application bar placed at the bottom of the screen. It usually contains some commands that are useful for interacting with the content of the current page.
- `TopAppBar` is used to define the application bar placed at the top of the screen. It provides the user quick access to the different sections of the applications. This way, the user can move to another section without going back to the home page. This property is available only in Windows.

The Windows Runtime includes two different controls to manage the application bar. Let's see in detail how they work.

CommandBar

The `CommandBar` control is ideal when you want to manage an application bar placed at the bottom of the page to provide some contextual features to the user. It a simple way to define a bar with a set of buttons that the user can press to trigger some functions.

The controls included in a `CommandBar` can be grouped into two different sections, which are managed with two different properties: `PrimaryCommands` and `SecondaryCommands`. The `CommandBar` control belongs to the optimized family; it works in the same way in both platforms, but it has a different look and feel. Let's see the main differences:

- In Windows, the two different sections define the side of the screen where the controls are placed. The primary commands are placed on the right side of the screen, while the secondary commands are placed on the left.
- In Windows Phone, the application bar can contain up to four buttons, which are the primary commands. They are always visible, and they are rendered with a text and an icon. The secondary commands are initially hidden; they are displayed only when the user expands the application bar by swiping it from the bottom of the screen or tapping on the ellipses on the right side of the application bar. The secondary commands are only textual; they don't have an icon like the primary commands.

Despite these differences, the CommandBar control is defined with the same XAML code on both platforms:

```
<Page
    x:Class="SampleApp.MainPage"
    xmlns="http://schemas.microsoft.com/winfx/2006/xaml/presentation"
    xmlns:x="http://schemas.microsoft.com/winfx/2006/xaml"
    xmlns:d="http://schemas.microsoft.com/expression/blend/2008"
    xmlns:mc="http://schemas.openxmlformats.org/markup-compatibility/2006"
    mc:Ignorable="d"
    Background="{ThemeResource ApplicationPageBackgroundThemeBrush}">

    <Page.BottomAppBar>
        <CommandBar>
            <CommandBar.PrimaryCommands>
                <!-- primary commands -->
            </CommandBar.PrimaryCommands>
            <CommandBar.SecondaryCommands>
                <!-- secondary commands -->
            </CommandBar.SecondaryCommands>
        </CommandBar>
    </Page.BottomAppBar>

    <Grid>
        <!-- page content -->
    </Grid>
</Page>
```

Inside a CommandBar, you can define three different type of commands (even if only one of them is supported by both platforms)

- A button, which is identified by the AppBarButton class.
- A toggle button (which is able to maintain the on/off state), identified by the AppBarToggleButton class. This control is supported only on Windows.
- A separator, which is useful to group the commands in different sections. It's identified by the AppBarSeparator class, and it's available only in Windows.

The buttons' visual layout is defined by two important properties: **Label** and **Icon**. Label is the text that is displayed below the button. **Icon** is the image that is displayed inside the button, and it works in a different way than a standard **Image** control. By default, in fact, you can't simply specify an image path, but one of the symbols that belong to the Segoe UI font family. You can find a list of all the available symbols in the MSDN documentation: http://s.qmatteoq.com/AppBarSymbols.

The following sample shows an **AppBarButton** control with a **Save** icon:

```
<Page.BottomAppBar>
    <CommandBar>
        <CommandBar.PrimaryCommands>
            <AppBarButton Label="Save" Icon="Save" />
        </CommandBar.PrimaryCommands>
    </CommandBar>
</Page.BottomAppBar>
```

If you can't find the right icon for you, there's still a way to use your own images as icons, by using the extended syntax to define the **Icon** property, like in the following sample:

```
<Page.BottomAppBar>
    <CommandBar>
        <CommandBar.PrimaryCommands>
            <AppBarButton Label="Save">
                <AppBarButton.Icon>
                    <BitmapIcon UriSource="/Assets/image.png" />
                </AppBarButton.Icon>
            </AppBarButton>
        </CommandBar.PrimaryCommands>
    </CommandBar>
</Page.BottomAppBar>
```

In a Windows Phone application, the **Icon** property will be ignored if the control is defined as a secondary command; only the text set in the **Label** property will be displayed.

When it comes to managing the user interaction with the application bar's commands, there are no differences compared to a regular **Button** control. They expose, in fact, a **Click** event, that you can subscribe in code behind to perform some operations when the button is clicked. The following code shows a complete **CommandBar** sample:

```
<Page.BottomAppBar>
    <CommandBar>
        <CommandBar.PrimaryCommands>
            <AppBarButton Label="refresh" Click="OnButton1Clicked"
Icon="Refresh" />
            <AppBarSeparator />
            <AppBarToggleButton Label="add" Click="OnButton2Clicked"
```

```
Icon="Favorite" />
        </CommandBar.PrimaryCommands>
        <CommandBar.SecondaryCommands>
            <AppBarButton Label="save" Click="OnButton3Clicked" Icon="Save"
/>
        </CommandBar.SecondaryCommands>
    </CommandBar>
</Page.BottomAppBar>
```

The following images show how this code is rendered differently on Windows and Windows Phone.

Figure 24: A CommandBar rendered on Windows

Figure 25: A CommandBar rendered on Windows Phone

AppBar (Windows only)

The **AppBar** control is available only on Windows, and it offers the maximum flexibility to the developer. Unlike the **CommandBar**, where you can add only some specific controls, it can contain any other XAML control, so that you can define your own layout. For this reason, it's typically used when you want to create a navigation bar that's placed at the top of the screen.

The following sample shows the XAML to define an **AppBar** control:

```
<Page.TopAppBar>
    <AppBar>
        <StackPanel Orientation="Horizontal">
            <Border Width="150" Height="150" Background="DarkGray"
Margin="20, 0, 20, 0">
                <Button Content="Section 1" HorizontalAlignment="Center"
VerticalAlignment="Center" Style="{StaticResource TextBlockButtonStyle}"
Click="OnSection1Clicked" />
            </Border>
            <Border Width="150" Height="150" Background="DarkGray"
Margin="20, 0, 20, 0">
                <Button Content="Section 2" HorizontalAlignment="Center"
VerticalAlignment="Center" Style="{StaticResource TextBlockButtonStyle}"
Click="OnSection2Clicked" />
            </Border>
            <Border Width="150" Height="150" Background="DarkGray"
Margin="20, 0, 20, 0">
                <Button Content="Section 3" HorizontalAlignment="Center"
VerticalAlignment="Center" Style="{StaticResource TextBlockButtonStyle}"
Click="OnSection3Clicked" />
            </Border>
        </StackPanel>
    </AppBar>
</Page.TopAppBar>
```

As you can see, there's nothing special to highlight; inside the **AppBar** control, you can place any XAML control you want. In the previous sample, the application bar contains three buttons (placed inside a square border) that are used to navigate to three different sections of the application.

Figure 26: An AppBar placed at the top of the application to provide quick navigation controls

StatusBar (Windows Phone only)

The **StatusBar** is another signature control that is available only in Windows Phone. It isn't really a control; it's the system tray placed at the top where the operating system shows some important information, like the time, the signal strength, etc. The Windows Runtime allows developers to interact with this bar to perform additional operations.

You can't interact with the status bar directly from the XAML, like you can in Windows Phone 8 and Silverlight. We need to manage it in the code behind, by using the **StatusBar** class (part of the **Windows.UI.ViewManagement** namespace), which offers a method called **GetForCurrentView()** that returns a reference to the bar.

Here are some of the main operations you can perform once you have a reference to the current bar:

Hiding and showing the status bar

As a developer, you're able to hide the status bar, so that the application can use all the available space on the screen. This feature can be useful also if your application is using a custom theme, which would look bad mixed together with the top bar, since by default it keeps the same theme color of the phone (black or white).

However, you have to be cautious in using this feature: hiding the status bar means that some important information will be hidden, unless the user decides to pull down the Action Center from the top of the screen. For example, if your application uses the data connection heavily, it's not a good idea to hide the status bar. If there are any issues, the user won't be able to notice immediately if they are caused by a network problem (for example, no cellular signal).

To hide the status bar, you can call the **HideAsync()** method, like in the following sample:

```
private async void OnChangeSystemTrayClicked(object sender, RoutedEventArgs e)
{
    StatusBar statusBar = StatusBar.GetForCurrentView();
    await statusBar.HideAsync();
}
```

If you want to display it again, just call the **ShowAsync()** method:

```
private async void OnChangeSystemTrayClicked(object sender, RoutedEventArgs e)
{
    StatusBar statusBar = StatusBar.GetForCurrentView();
    await statusBar.ShowAsync();
}
```

Changing the look and feel

If you don't want to hide the bar, but you still don't want your application to look bad because the status bar color doesn't mix well with your theme, the **StatusBar** control offers more choices.

One approach is to change the bar's opacity. You'll be able to make it transparent, so that the various indicators (time, signal strength, etc.) will still be visible, but will be displayed over your application's theme without interfering with it. To achieve this goal, you need to set the **BackgroundOpacity** property with the opacity value you prefer, like in the following sample:

```
private void OnChangeSystemTrayClicked(object sender, RoutedEventArgs e)
{
    StatusBar statusBar = StatusBar.GetForCurrentView();
    statusBar.BackgroundOpacity = 0.4;
}
```

Another approach, used in combination with the **BackgroundOpacity** property we've seen before, is to change the background color by setting the **BackgroundColor** property, like in the following sample:

```
private void OnChangeSystemTrayClicked(object sender, RoutedEventArgs e)
{
    StatusBar statusBar = StatusBar.GetForCurrentView();
    statusBar.BackgroundOpacity = 1.0;
    statusBar.BackgroundColor = Colors.Red;
}
```

Showing a progress bar

Previously in this chapter, we learned how to use controls such **ProgressBar** and
ProgressRing to display the status of a running operation to the user. However, there's another
alternative on Windows Phone: instead of showing a progress bar inside the page, you can
display it in the status bar on the top of the screen. In this case, you need to use the
ProgressIndicator control, which, like the **ProgressBar** control, supports two kind of
animations. The default is an indeterminate animation, which is used to keep track of operations
for which you aren't able to determine the exact duration. Otherwise, if you want to display a
standard progress bar, you can fill the **ProgressValue** property with a value between **0** (empty
bar) and **1** (full bar).

Regardless of the behavior you choose, you can add also a text using the **Text** property, which
is displayed below the progress bar, like in the following sample:

```
private async void OnChangeSystemTrayClicked(object sender, RoutedEventArgs
e)
{
    StatusBar statusBar = StatusBar.GetForCurrentView();
    statusBar.ProgressIndicator.Text = "Loading...";
    await statusBar.ProgressIndicator.ShowAsync();
}
```

Once you've configured the **ProgessIndicator** property exposed by the **StatusBar** control,
you can display it by calling the **ShowAsync()** method, or hide it by using the **HideAsync()**
method.

Chapter 4 The Core Concepts: Resolutions, Navigation, and App Life Cycle

Managing Resolutions and Screen Sizes

One distinctive feature of Windows Store apps is that they can run on multiple devices including smartphones, tablets, and traditional computers. However, each of them offers different form factors and screen sizes. In the Windows ecosystem, smartphones usually have screens from 3.5 to six inches while tablets offer screens from seven to 12 inches. Desktop computers, on the other hand, can be connected to 30-inch or larger monitors.

Consequently, when we create our app's UI, we can't use a fixed layout; we need to keep in mind that layout should be able to automatically adapt to the device's form factor and provide a good UI, no matter on which kind of device an app is running.

Both Windows and Windows Phone support virtually any screen size and resolution, which typically fall into two categories: devices with a 15:9 aspect ratio (such as the WXGA or WVGA resolutions) and devices with a 16:9 aspect ratio (such as the 720p and 1080p resolutions).

However, you can't rely on these fixed values to define your layout as these resolutions can change in the future (since the Windows Runtime is much more flexible than Silverlight in supporting different resolutions and screen sizes). In this section, we'll look at the best strategies to design a layout that can properly adapt to virtually any device.

How Scaling Works

Windows and Windows Phone offer a native scaling system which is able to automatically adapt a page's layout according to the screen's size and resolution. This is possible thanks to the XAML framework, which is a vector-based technology. XAML controls are represented by a series of dots and lines. This way, when the resolution of the device increases, the OS is able to increase the size of the elements in a page without losing quality.

This increase is performed by using a scale factor, which is calculated as the ratio between the pixel size and the real size of the screen. It's a huge improvement compared to the scale system that was applied by Silverlight in Windows Phone 8.0, which was calculated only according to the resolution. The downside was that the layout of the page wasn't able to automatically adapt to the screen's size. For instance, on a big device (such as a phablet), the content's density was the same as it was displayed on a smaller device. The only difference was that the elements in the page were just bigger (so, bigger fonts, bigger buttons, bigger images, etc.). In the end, the UX was compromised because the app wasn't able to make use of the wider space offered by bigger devices.

The Windows Runtime offers many different scale factors. According to the resolution and the size of the screen, the XAML elements displayed in a page are multiplied for a fixed value, which makes things easier to read and for the user to interact with.

The standard scale factors offered by Windows 8.1 are:

- 1.0 is the base scaling factor, which is supported by devices with a minimum resolution of 1024x768
- 1.4 introduces a 140 percent scale factor, which is supported by devices with a minimum resolution of 1440x1080
- 1.8 introduces a 180 percent scale factor, which is supported by devices with a minimum resolution of 1920x1440

Windows Phone 8.1 uses the following scale factors:

- 1.0 is the base scale factor, which is applied to the minimum resolution supported by Windows Phone devices, which is 384x640
- 1.4 introduces a 140 percent scale factor
- 2.4 introduces a 240 percent scale factor and it's applied to devices such as phablets that have big screen sizes and high resolution

 It's important to highlight that the minimum resolutions mentioned in the previous lists are just an indication. It isn't necessary, for example, that a device with a 1440x1080 resolution have a 1.4 scale factory since it's calculated also according to other parameters such as the screen's size. The Surface Pro is a good example of this behavior; it has a 1920x1080 resolution but, since it's a 10-inch device, it has a 1.4 scale factor.

The Windows Runtime offers a class called `DisplayProperties`, which is useful to determine the applied scale factor thanks to the `ResolutionScale` property. The following code sample shows the user the current scale factor applied to his or her device:

```
protected override void OnNavigatedTo(NavigationEventArgs e)
{
    ResolutionScale scale = DisplayProperties.ResolutionScale;
    string description = string.Empty;
    switch (scale)
    {
        case ResolutionScale.Scale100Percent:
            description = "Scale factor: 100";
            break;
        case ResolutionScale.Scale140Percent:
            description = "Scale factor: 140";
            break;
        case ResolutionScale.Scale180Percent:
            description = "Scale factor: 180";
            break;
    }

    ScaleFactor.Text = description;
}
```

Managing the Layout

When it comes to defining the layout of the app, the XAML framework helps us. Since it's a vector-based technology, it's able to automatically adapt to the screen's size and resolution without losing quality. However, that doesn't mean that there aren't any precautions to keep in mind. The most important one is to avoid assigning a fixed size to our controls. In fact, when you give a fixed size to a control, it's not able to automatically fill the available space. Consequently, it's important to avoid using controls such as **Canvas** and **Border** when you define the layout since they work with an absolute positioning. The content isn't able to automatically fit the container but, instead, they're placed in a fixed position by using properties such as **Top** and **Left**. On the contrary, the **Grid** control is the best container that you can use to define a fluid layout. As we've seen in Chapter 3, you're able to define rows and columns whose size is able to automatically adapt to the content.

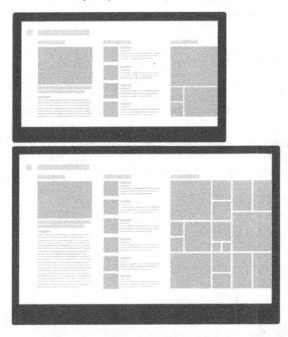

Figure 1: A fluid layout sample: On a bigger screen, the app is able to display more content than on a smaller screen

However, there are some scenarios in which this approach can lead to some issues, especially in games. For example, let's consider a chess game. The number of squares on a chessboard is fixed no matter the size of the device. In a scenario such as this, we don't need to display more content if the screen is bigger, we just need to display the content with a bigger size. In these situations, we can use the **ViewBox** control which is able to automatically scale the content according to the screen's size. On bigger devices, the content will simply look bigger but the content's density will be always the same.

It is easy to use this control: just wrap inside it the XAML controls you want to automatically scale, like in the following sample:

```
<Viewbox>
    <StackPanel>
        <TextBlock Text="Some text" />
        <TextBlock Text="Some other text" />
    </StackPanel>
</Viewbox>
```

Managing Images

When working with images, we don't have the same flexibility offered by the XAML framework. In fact, images are rendered as bitmaps, not as vectors, so the more the image size is increased, the bigger the quality loss is. To manage images, Windows Store apps offer a naming convention that greatly helps developers to support all of the devices. You will need to add different versions of the images (with different resolutions) and the Windows Runtime will automatically pick the best one according to the device's scale factor.

For example, let's say that you have an image with a 100x100 resolution. To properly support all of the possible screen sizes and resolutions, we will have to also add to the project the same image with a 140x140 resolution (for the 1.4 scale factor), an image with a 180x180 resolution (for the 1.8 scale factor) and an image with a 240x240 resolution (for the 2.4 scale factor). There are two ways to manage this scenario and they both produce the same result. It's up to you to choose which one best fits your needs and your coding habits.

The first way is to include the images in the same folder but with a name that ends with a different suffix. For example, if the original image is called **logo.png**, you will have to add the following files:

- **logo.scale-100.png** for the 1.0 scale factor
- **logo.scale-140.png** for the 1.4 scale factor
- **logo.scale-180.png** for the 1.8 scale factor
- **logo.scale-240.png** for the 2.4 scale factor

The second way requires you to always use the same file name but store it in different folders. For example, if the original image is called **logo.png**, you will have to organize the project with the following folders:

- **/scale-100/logo.png** for the 1.0 scale factor
- **/scale-140/logo.png** for the 1.4 scale factor
- **/scale-180/logo.png** for the 1.8 scale factor
- **/scale-240/logo.png** for the 2.4 scale factor

The most important thing to highlight is that this approach is completely transparent to the developer. You'll simply have to assign to your control the base name of the image and the Windows Runtime will take care of picking up the best image for you. For example, to display the previous image called **logo.png** by using an **Image** control, you will have just to declare the following code:

```
<Image Source="/Assets/logo.png" />
```

The Windows Store app will automatically use the proper version of the image according to the current scale factor.

Managing External Images

Of course, the previous approach only works for images that are part of the Visual Studio's project. If the image is downloaded from the web, you'll have to manually manage the different versions of the image. You can rely on the **ResolutionScale** property offered by the **DisplayProperties** class we've seen before to achieve this goal; you'll be able to retrieve the proper scale factor and download the proper image for your device.

Managing the Visual Assets

The approach we have just discussed regarding images is also applied to the standard visual assets required by any Windows Store app (such as icons, tiles, etc.). If you have read Chapter 2, you would remember that the standard visual assets of the app are defined inside the manifest file, in a specific section called **Visual Assets**. You will notice that, for every image requested in the section, you'll be able to load multiple versions of them to support the different scale factors. The visual manifest editor will help you to understand the proper resolution to use when you define the image to use. For example, if you look at the Splash screen section in the Windows manifest file, you'll notice that, under every image, the proper resolution required for every specific scale factor is reported:

- The base image, with scale factor 1.0, should have a 620x300 resolution
- The image with scale factor 1.4 should have an 868x420 resolution
- The image with scale factor 1.8 should have a 1116x540 resolution

Let's take a look, in detail, at the different kind of images that are required in the manifest file.

Tile Images and Logos

This section is used to define the logo of the app. Multiple formats are required and each of them corresponds to a specific use case. Let's look at them in detail:

- The small square tile is managed in different ways in Windows and Windows Phone. On Windows, the image is defined in the section titled **Square70x70 Logo**. On Windows Phone, it's defined in the **Square71x71 Logo** section.
- **Square150x150 Logo** is the image used for the standard square tile.
- **Wide310x150 Logo** is the image used for the wide rectangular tile.
- **Square310x310 Logo** is a section available only on Windows. It's the image used for the big square tile which is not available on Windows Phone.
- There are some pages, in the OS, on which a smaller logo is required (such as in the app list). Again, the size is different according to the platform. On Windows, it's defined in the **Square30x30 Logo** section. On Windows Phone, it's defined in the **Square44x44 Logo** section.

Badge Logo

Windows Store apps can also interact with the user on the lock screen, which is displayed when the user is not actively using the device. The most common scenario are notifications. We can alert the user that something happened in the app (for example, the user received a new email message) without forcing them to unlock his or her device. In this section, you'll be able to define the image that will be used to display such notifications. The main requirement of this image is that it has to be monochromatic and have a transparent background.

Splash Screen

The splash screen image is displayed to the user when the app is loading. As soon as the loading is completed, the splash screen is hidden and the first page of the app is displayed. There is an important difference in how the splash screen is implemented on both platforms:

- In Windows 8.1, the splash screen image is displayed at the center of the screen and it doesn't fill all the available space (in fact, the requested resolution is 620x300, which is less than any resolution supported by any Windows device). Consequently, you are also able to set a background color which will fill the remaining space. To obtain the best result, it's important that the color matches the color of the image used as the splash screen.
- In Windows Phone 8.1, the splash screen image uses the entire screen space so the background color property is missing.

How to Test Scaling

It can be tricky to test to see whether or not you have properly managed the layout and the images of your app so that it can perform well (no matter which device the app is running on). You would require access to many devices, each of them with different resolutions and screen sizes. Luckily, Visual Studio 2013 offers some tools that can help the developer to simulate different scale factors.

When it comes to a Windows app, you can use the simulator we've described in Chapter 1. In fact, it offers an option in the toolbar that is able to change the current resolution and screen's size for of the simulator.

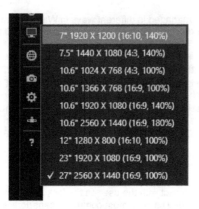

Figure 2: The different resolution and screen sizes offered by the Windows simulator

When it comes to Windows Phone, Visual Studio offers you the chance to run different versions of the emulator from the Debug drop-down menu, as you can see in the following image:

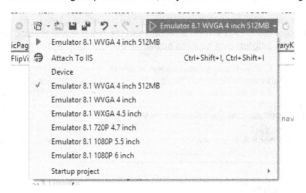

Figure 3: The different emulators available in Visual Studio 2013

Windows Store Apps Side-by-Side (Windows only)

One of the most interesting features in Windows is that the user is able to run multiple Windows Store apps at the same time by placing them side-by-side. In most cases, users are able to place two apps side-by-side but the number isn't fixed, it's up to the resolution and the screen size of the device. This scenario is only supported by Windows. Smartphones, since they typically offer smaller screens, would offer a poor UX.

As developers, it's important to learn to manage this feature. At any time, the user could resize the size of our app and we need to be ready to provide a good UX at any size. This Windows feature is deeply changed during the transition from Windows 8.0 to Windows 8.1. In fact, in the first Windows 8 version, we were required to manage only three different states:

- **Snapped:** the app uses approximately 1/3 of the screen
- **Filled**: the app uses approximately 2/3 of the screen so that it can be placed side-by-side to a snapped app
- **Full screen**: the app is regularly running using the entire available space on the screen

In Windows 8.1, instead, the user can assign to an app virtually any size, as long as the device supports at least a 1024x768 resolution. The new minimum size that a Windows Store app can assume is 500 pixels; however, as developers, we can still enable the old snapped mode by setting the **Minimum Width** property in the manifest file (in the **Application** section) to 320 pixels. The choice is up to the developer. According to the type of content displayed by the app, you have to ask yourself if you'll be able to display the content even with such a small window or if would become useless or unreadable.

For example, a Twitter client is a type of app that can support the snapped view just fine. This way, the user could snap his or her timeline to the side and, for example, keep surfing the web while keeping an eye on Twitter. This is because the timeline is a type of content that doesn't require too much space in order to be properly rendered. On the other hand, a game typically wouldn't be able to properly support a snapped view since it would be hard to play it at such a small size.

Whether or not we want to enable snapped view, as developers and designers we need to follow the same rule we learned when we talked about managing the different resolutions and screen sizes: keeping the layout fluid. The more fluid the layout is, the better it will be able to adapt to the size of the window. However, there are some scenarios in which this approach isn't enough. In some cases, the content of the page can become too small to be meaningful if the size of the windows is reduced too much.

A solution to this problem is offered by the visual states we've described in Chapter 3. We're going to define different visual states and each of them will reflect the various states that the app can assume. When we reach a window size that is no longer suitable to display our content correctly, we're going to deeply change the layout of the page. We're going to use, as an example, the same scenario we talked in Chapter 3 regarding `GridView` and `ListView` controls: a collection of people grouped by the city in which they live.

Let's take a look at how our page looks:

```
<Page
x:Class="App1.MainPage"
xmlns="http://schemas.microsoft.com/winfx/2006/xaml/presentation"
xmlns:x="http://schemas.microsoft.com/winfx/2006/xaml"
xmlns:local="using:App1"
xmlns:d="http://schemas.microsoft.com/expression/blend/2008"
xmlns:mc="http://schemas.openxmlformats.org/markup-compatibility/2006"
mc:Ignorable="d">

    <Page.Resources>
```

```xml
        <CollectionViewSource x:Name="People" IsSourceGrouped="True" />

        <DataTemplate x:Key="PeopleTemplate">
            <StackPanel Width="300">
                <TextBlock Text="{Binding Path=Name}" />
                <TextBlock Text="{Binding Path=Surname}" />
            </StackPanel>
        </DataTemplate>

        <DataTemplate x:Key="HeaderTemplate">
            <Border Background="LightGray">
                <TextBlock Text="{Binding Key}" Foreground="Black" Margin="10"
Style="{StaticResource HeaderTextBlockStyle}"/>
            </Border>
        </DataTemplate>
    </Page.Resources>

    <Grid Background="{ThemeResource ApplicationPageBackgroundThemeBrush}">
        <VisualStateManager.VisualStateGroups>
            <VisualStateGroup>
                <VisualState x:Name="DefaultLayout" />
                <VisualState x:Name="MinimalLayout">
                    <Storyboard>
                        <ObjectAnimationUsingKeyFrames
Storyboard.TargetName="GridPeople" Storyboard.TargetProperty="Visibility">
                            <DiscreteObjectKeyFrame KeyTime="0" Value="Collapsed" />
                        </ObjectAnimationUsingKeyFrames>
                        <ObjectAnimationUsingKeyFrames
Storyboard.TargetName="ListPeople" Storyboard.TargetProperty="Visibility">
                            <DiscreteObjectKeyFrame KeyTime="0" Value="Visible" />
                        </ObjectAnimationUsingKeyFrames>
                    </Storyboard>
                </VisualState>
            </VisualStateGroup>
        </VisualStateManager.VisualStateGroups>
        <GridView ItemsSource="{Binding Source={StaticResource People}}"
x:Name="GridPeople" ItemTemplate="{StaticResource PeopleTemplate}">
            <GridView.GroupStyle>
                <GroupStyle HidesIfEmpty="True" HeaderTemplate="{StaticResource
HeaderTemplate}" />
            </GridView.GroupStyle>
        </GridView>
        <ListView ItemsSource="{Binding Source={StaticResource People}}"
Visibility="Collapsed" x:Name="ListPeople" ItemTemplate="{StaticResource
PeopleTemplate}">
            <ListView.GroupStyle>
                <GroupStyle HidesIfEmpty="True" HeaderTemplate="{StaticResource
HeaderTemplate}" />
            </ListView.GroupStyle>
        </ListView>
    </Grid>
</Page>
```

We've added two controls in the page: a GridView and a ListView, both configured to display the same data (which is the CollectionViewSource defined as a page resource). Also, the look and feel is the same; they both use the same templates to render a single item (the person) and the group header (the city name). You will also notice that, by default, the GridView control is visible while the ListView one is hidden (the Visibility property is set to Collapsed).

The goal of our work is to change the layout of the page when the user resizes the app to a point so that the GridView isn't able to fulfill anymore its job (which is to properly display the data). When we reach that point, we're going to hide the GridView and replace it with the ListView. Since it features a vertical layout, it fits best the scenario in which the size of the app is smaller.

To achieve our goal, we have defined two different visual states inside the main Grid container: the first one is called DefaultLayout which identifies the base status (the GridView is visible, while the ListView is hidden). The second one is called MinimalLayout and it does the opposite (the GridView is hidden, while the ListView is made visible).

Now that we have defined the visual states, let's take a look at how to manage the code behind the switch:

```
public sealed partial class MainPage : Page
{
    public MainPage()
    {
        this.InitializeComponent();
        this.SizeChanged += MainPage_SizeChanged;
    }

    private void MainPage_SizeChanged(object sender, SizeChangedEventArgs e)
    {
        if (e.NewSize.Width <= 500)
        {
            VisualStateManager.GoToState(this, "MinimalLayout", true);
        }
        else
        {
            VisualStateManager.GoToState(this, "DefaultLayout", true);
        }
    }
}
```

In the page's constructor, we've subscribed to the SizeChanged event, which is invoked when the user changes the size of the app. The event handler's parameter contains a property called NewSize which returns the new size of the window. Since Windows Store apps can only be resized horizontally, we are interested in checking the value of the Width property.

Now it's our turn to define the critical point that, when reached, will force the layout to change. In the previous sample, we've set it to 500 pixels. When this value is reached, we enable the `MinimalLayout` visual state by using the `GoToState()` method exposed by the `VisualStateManager` class. Otherwise, if the user decides to resize the app again and increase the size to a value higher than 500 pixels, we restore the original visual state called `DefaultLayout`.

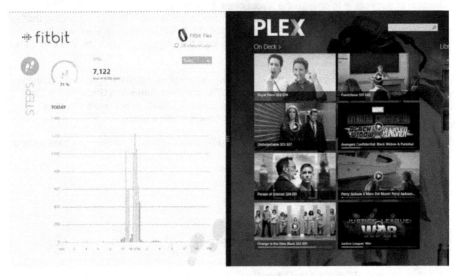

Figure 4: Two Windows Store apps running side-by-side

Managing Orientation

The approach previously described to manage the app resizing can also be applied to orientation management, which is supported not only by Windows but also by Windows Phone. In fact, on both platforms devices can be used horizontally (landscape mode) or vertically (portrait mode). Managing both orientations is not required but it's a bonus that is appreciated by users.

Windows Store apps are able to automatically manage the orientation change. The first step is to enable, in the manifest file, the orientations you want to support. Then, the app is able to automatically rotate the page's content when the device changes orientation. However, this approach doesn't always provide good results as working with visual states is the best way to manage the orientation change. This way, we can manually change the layout of the app according to the way the user is holding the device.

From the XAML point of view, the code is the same as we've seen in the app's resize sample. You define two visual states (one for the portrait and one for the landscape) in which you're going to set how the controls will look according to the orientation.

The main difference is in the code behind; we'll need to manage the **SizeChanged** event in a different way, like in the following sample:

```
public sealed partial class MainPage : Page
{
    public MainPage()
    {
        this.InitializeComponent();
        this.SizeChanged += MainPage_SizeChanged;
    }
    private void MainPage_SizeChanged(object sender, SizeChangedEventArgs e)
    {
        if (e.NewSize.Width > e.NewSize.Height)
        {
            VisualStateManager.GoToState(this, "DefaultLayout", true);
        }
        else
        {
            VisualStateManager.GoToState(this, "PortraitLayout", true);
        }
    }
}
```

The **SizeChanged** event is also triggered when the orientation of the device changes. In this case, we can use the **Width** and **Height** properties offered by the **NewSize** parameter to determine the current orientation. If the **Width** is higher than the **Height**, it means that the device is being used in landscape mode; otherwise, it's being used in portrait mode. By using the **VisualStateManager**, we trigger the proper visual state according to this condition.

Both the Windows simulator and the Windows Phone emulator can help us to test this scenario by providing us with an option to rotate the device.

Navigation in Windows Store Apps

As we've previously mentioned in this book, unlike traditional desktop apps, Windows Store apps are based on pages. Every page displays some content and the user can navigate from one page to another to explore the app. Consequently, Windows Store apps are based on the **Frame** concept which is the container of all the app pages. A **Frame** can contain one or more **Page** objects which are managed with a hierarchy similar to the one offered by websites: the user has the chance to move back and forth across the different pages.

The Page's Life Cycle

As we've already seen, every app's page inherits from the **Page** class which offers a set of events that are important to manage the page's life cycle. In this book, we'll often use two of them: **OnNavigatedTo()** and **OnNavigatedFrom()**. The first one is triggered when the user navigates to the current page; it's one of the best entry points to initialize the data that needs to be displayed in the page (for example, to retrieve some data from a database or a web service). The second one is triggered when the user navigates away from the current page to another one. We're going to use these two events, in the next paragraphs, to save and restore the page's state so that we can properly manage the app's life cycle.

```
protected override void OnNavigatedTo(NavigationEventArgs e)
{
    //load the data
}
protected override void OnNavigatedFrom(NavigationEventArgs e)
{
    //save the data
}
```

Navigating across Pages

Since it's the pages' container, the **Frame** class offers the basic methods with which to perform navigation from one page to another. The basic one is called **Navigate()** and it accepts, as parameter, the type that identifies the page to where you want to redirect the user.

For example, if you want to redirect the user to a page called MainPage.xaml, with a type called **MainPage**, you can use the following code:

```
private void OnGoToMainPageClicked(object sender, RoutedEventArgs e)
{
    this.Frame.Navigate(typeof(MainPage));
}
```

The **Navigate()** method also accepts a second parameter, which is an object that you want to pass from one page to another. It's useful in common master–detail scenarios in which the user taps on an element in one page and he or she is redirected to another page to see more information about the selected item.

The following sample code retrieves the selected item from a **ListView** control and passes it to another page:

```
private void OnGoToMainPageClicked(object sender, RoutedEventArgs e)
{
    Person person = People.SelectedItem as Person;
    this.Frame.Navigate(typeof(MainPage), person);
```

```
}
```

Next, we're able to retrieve the parameter in the **OnNavigateTo()** event handler of the destination page, thanks to the **Parameter** property stored in the navigation parameters, like in the following sample:

```
protected override async void OnNavigatedTo(NavigationEventArgs e)
{
    Person person = e.Parameter as Person;
    MessageDialog dialog = new MessageDialog(person.Name);
    await dialog.ShowAsync();
}
```

Since the **Parameter** property can contain a generic **object**, we need to first perform a cast to the expected type. However, it's important to highlight that the object passed as parameter should be serializable, which means that it can be represented by a plain string. We'll talk again about this important concept in Chapter 5.

Managing the Page Stack

Windows Store apps follow a hierarchical approach when it comes to navigation, which is very similar to the one offered by web apps. Typically, the user starts from a main page and then he or she moves to the other pages of the app. However, the user can also decide to navigate backwards and move back to the previous pages.

Even if the concept is the same, Windows and Windows Phone manage this requirement in two different ways. In fact, Windows Phone devices always offer a real **Back** button (which can be physical or virtual) that is part of the platform's UX. Windows devices don't offer such a configuration, mainly for two reasons:

- Tablets are bigger than smartphones so a physical **Back** button can be hard to reach while holding them
- Windows Store apps can run not just on tablets but also on traditional computers, which are controlled with a standard keyboard and mouse configuration

The page hierarchy is managed like a stack: every time you navigate to a new page, a new item is added at the top of the stack. When you navigate back, the page at the top of the stack is removed. Despite this difference, both platforms requires the developer to properly manage the backward navigation by using the **GoBack()** button offered by the **Frame** class.

However, you'll have to manage it in two different ways due to the hardware differences. Let's look at these in detail.

Managing the Back Button in Windows

As we've already highlighted, Windows devices don't provide a real **Back** button, so you'll have to manage it in your apps. The standard Visual Studio templates (except for the blank one) already support this scenario; every page contains, near the header, a `Button` control with the following features:

- It invokes the `GoBack()` method of the Frame class when it's clicked.
- It's displayed only if the `CanGoBack` property of the `Frame` class is set to **true**. This property checks the status of the page's stack and it is set to **true** only if there is at least one page available to go back to.

This is a sample that performs this operation:

```
private void OnGoBackClicked(object sender, RoutedEventArgs e)
{
    if (Frame.CanGoBack)
    {
        Frame.GoBack();
    }
}
```

Managing the Back Button in Windows Phone

Windows Phone offers a dedicated **Back** button. In Windows Phone 8, as a developer, you didn't have to do anything special to properly manage it. Automatically, when it was pressed, the user was redirected to the previous page of the app (or to the Start screen in case the stack was empty and the user was in the first page of the app).

This behavior isn't automatically implemented anymore in Windows Phone 8.1. When you press **Back**, the user won't be redirected to the previous page anymore but, instead, will be redirected to the previously used app to keep the navigation consistent with the one offered by Windows (since it doesn't offer a dedicated **Back** button). However, it doesn't mean that this is the proper way to manage the **Back** button. Windows Phone users are used to moving through the different app's sections by using the **Back** button and Microsoft wants to keep it this way.

As such, all the Visual Studio templates (except the Blank one) include a class in the Common folder called `NavigationHelper` which provides many useful features—especially to manage the page state (we'll talk about this later in this chapter in detail). One of the features offered by this class is a proper support of the **Back** button. The class, in fact, contains the following code:

```
public class NavigationHelper
{
    private Page Page { get; set; }
    private Frame Frame { get { return this.Page.Frame; } }

    public NavigationHelper(Page page)
    {
        this.Page = page;
        this.Page.Loaded += (sender, e) =>
```

```
            {
#if WINDOWS_PHONE_APP
            Windows.Phone.UI.Input.HardwareButtons.BackPressed +=
HardwareButtons_BackPressed;
#endif
        };
        this.Page.Unloaded += (sender, e) =>
        {
#if WINDOWS_PHONE_APP
            Windows.Phone.UI.Input.HardwareButtons.BackPressed -=
HardwareButtons_BackPressed;
#endif
        };
    }

    private void HardwareButtons_BackPressed(object sender, Windows.Phone.
    UI.Input.BackPressedEventArgs e)
    {
        if (this.Frame.CanGoBack)
        {
            e.Handled = true;
            this.Frame.GoBack();
        }
    }
}
```

When the class is instantiated, it subscribes to the **BackPressed** event offered by the **HardwareButtons** class that is part of the **Windows.Phone.UI.Input** namespace. As the name suggests, the event is triggered every time the **Back** button in Windows Phone is pressed. The associated event handler simply takes care of calling the **GoBack()** method offered by the **Frame** class. The only line of code to highlight is **e.Handled = true**. By doing this, we're telling the OS that we've managed the **Back** button by ourselves. This way, Windows Phone won't try to manage it by itself and won't redirect the user to the previous app.

To use this class, we need to create a new **NavigationHelper** instance in the page constructor, like in the following sample:

```
public sealed partial class MainPage : Page
{
    public MainPage()
    {
        this.InitializeComponent();
        NavigationHelper helper = new NavigationHelper(this);
    }
}
```

However, if you're going to use any Visual Studio template (except Blank Page) to create new pages, the previous code will be automatically included.

If, by any chance, you need to manage the **Back** button in a different way, it's enough not to initialize the `NavigationHelper` class in your page and subscribe by yourself to the `BackPressed` event, like in the following sample:

```
public sealed partial class MainPage : Page
{
    public MainPage()
    {
        this.InitializeComponent();
        Windows.Phone.Input.UI.HardwareButtons.BackPressed +=
HardwareButtons_BackPressed;
    }

    void HardwareButtons_BackPressed(object sender, BackPressedEventArgs e)
    {
        //do something
        e.Handled = true;
    }
}
```

Avoiding the Circular Navigation Issue in Windows Phone

One really important thing to manage when you work with the page stack is to always use the `GoBack()` method of the `Frame` class when you want to redirect the user to the previous page; never use the `Navigate()` one.

This is required since, as we've previously mentioned, pages are managed with a stack. The `GoBack()` method removes the top page in the stack while the `Navigate()` adds a new one to the top. The result is that, if we use the `Navigate()` method to go back to the previous page, we create a circular navigation where the user keeps moving between the same two pages.

Let's look at a real example. Let's say that you have an app with a main page which displays a list of news. The app offers a Settings button that redirects the user to a page where the user can configure the app. At the bottom of this page, we have added a Confirm button. When it's tapped, the settings are saved and the user is redirected back to the main page.

Let's say that we perform this backward navigation to the main page by using the `Navigate()` method. What happens is, instead of removing the Settings page from the stack, we add the Main page on the top of it. The result is that, if the user now presses **Back** instead of returning to the Start menu (which is the expected behavior since the user is on the main page), the user will be redirected back to the Settings page since it's already present in the stack.

The proper way to manage this scenario is to call the `GoBack()` method when the user presses **Confirm**. This way, the Settings page will be removed from the stack, leaving the Main page as the only available page in the stack. This way, pressing **Back** again will correctly redirect the user to the Start screen, quitting the app.

Managing the Page's State

If you've already worked with Windows Phone 8.0 and Silverlight, you'll notice a very important difference when it comes to managing the page state. In Windows Phone 8.0, until a page was removed from the stack, its state was kept in memory. This means that, if the user pressed **Back** to go back to the previous page, he or she would have found the page in the same state as he or she previously left it.

This doesn't happen anymore in Windows Store apps, both for Windows and Windows Phone. Now, whenever the user is redirected to a page (no matter if it's a forward navigation to a new page or a backward navigation to a page already in the stack), a new instance is created. This means that the state is never maintained. If, for example, a page contains a **TextBox** control and the user writes something in it, as soon as he or she moves away from the page, that content will be lost.

If you want to avoid this issue and keep the previous behavior, you can set the **NavigationCacheMode** property of the page to **Required** or **Enabled** in the page constructor or in the XAML code. This way, the page state will always be maintained. It's important to highlight that, in this case, you'll need to properly manage the data loading and avoiding loading things in the page constructor since it gets called only the first time the page is requested. It's better to use methods such as **OnNavigatedTo()**, which are triggered every time the user navigates to the page. What is the difference between the two values? They both preserve the page's state but **Required** uses more memory since it will always cache the page no matter how many other pages have already been cached. With **Enabled**, the page will be cached but, if the cache size limit is hit, the state will be deleted.

The following sample shows how to set the **NavigationCacheMode** property:

```
public sealed partial class MainPage : Page
{
    public MainPage()
    {
        this.InitializeComponent();
        this.NavigationCacheMode = NavigationCacheMode.Required;
    }
}
```

The App's Life Cycle

One of the biggest differences between a Windows Store app and a traditional Windows desktop app is the life cycle, which means the different states that the app can assume while it's running. Usually, the life cycle of traditional desktop apps is quite simple since they are limited only by the hardware on which the app is running. The app is started and it always stays active until the user closes it, without any limitation about the chances to perform background operations.

However, this approach doesn't fit well with mobile apps as performance, low battery usage, and responsiveness are key factors on moibile platforms. The freedom offered by standard desktop apps doesn't respect these requirements.

Windows Store apps aren't always running; when the user switches to another activity (such as opening another app or moving back to the Start screen), the app is suspended. Its state is preserved in memory but it's not running anymore so it doesn't use any resources (such as CPU, network, etc.). Consequently, when an app is suspended, it's not able to perform background operations. For this purpose, the Windows Runtime has introduced background tasks (which will be detailed in Chapter 11). In most cases, the suspension management is transparent to the developer; when the user resumes our app, it will simply be restored along with its state. This way, the user will find the app in the same state that he or she previously left it.

However, devices (especially tablets and smartphones) don't have unlimited memory. Consequently, the OS is able to terminate the older apps in case it's running out of resources. As developers, it's important to save the state of the app during suspend so that we can restore it in case the app is terminated by the system. The goal is to offer a fluid experience to the user: he or she should always find the app in the same state he or she left, no matter if the app was just suspended or terminated.

It's important not to confuse the app's state (for example, the content of a form that the user is filling out and which he or she doesn't want to lose, even if he or she switches to another task) with the app's data (such as a database). As we will learn in Chapter 5, an app's data should be saved as soon as it's changed in order to minimize data loss in case something goes wrong (such as an unexpected crash of the app).

Let's take a look, in detail, at the different states of the app's life cycle.

Launching

All the Windows Store apps start from a base state called **NotRunning** which means that the app hasn't been launched yet. When the app is started from this state, the launching event is triggered, which takes care of initializing the frame and the main page. Once the app is initialized, it's moved to the **Running** state.

A Windows Store app is able to manage the life cycle events in the **App** class defined in the App.xaml.cs file. Specifically, the launching event is called **OnLaunched()**. It's triggered only when the app is initialized from scratch because it wasn't already running or suspended.

The following code show a typical launching management:

```
protected override void OnLaunched(LaunchActivatedEventArgs e)
{
    Frame rootFrame = Window.Current.Content as Frame;

    // Do not repeat app initialization when the Window already has content;
    // just ensure that the window is active
    if (rootFrame == null)
    {
        // Create a frame to act as the navigation context and navigate to the first
page
```

```
        rootFrame = new Frame();

        // TODO: change this value to a cache size that is appropriate for your
application
        rootFrame.CacheSize = 1;

        if (e.PreviousExecutionState == ApplicationExecutionState.Terminated)
        {
            // TODO: Load state from previously suspended application
        }

        // Place the frame in the current Window
        Window.Current.Content = rootFrame;
    }

    if (rootFrame.Content == null)
    {
        // When the navigation stack isn't restored, navigate to the first page,
        // configuring the new page by passing required information as a navigation
        // parameter
        if (!rootFrame.Navigate(typeof(MainPage), e.Arguments))
        {
            throw new Exception("Failed to create initial page");
        }
    }

    // Ensure the current window is active
    Window.Current.Activate();
}
```

The most important part of the previous code is the check of the **PreviousExecutionState** property which is one of the properties offered by the event's parameters. This property can assume different states according to the previous status of the app. Typically, in the launching event, you'll be able to catch the following states:

- **NotRunning**, which means that it's the first time the app is launched
- **Terminated**, which means that the app was already in memory but it's been terminated by the OS due to low resources
- **ClosedByUser**, which means that the app was already in memory but it's been terminated by the user

By default, the standard **App** class code suggests to manage the **Terminated** state: the app has been killed by the OS so it's our duty, as developers, to restore the state we've previously saved. We'll take a look at the proper ways to do this later in this chapter. As you can see, the two other states (**NotRunning** and **ClosedByUser**) are not managed: the app wasn't running or it has been explicitly closed by the user so it's correct to start it from scratch, without restoring any previous state.

Suspending

As already mentioned, the suspending event is triggered when the user decides to perform another task such as opening another app, tapping on a notification, or returning to the Start screen. When such an event occurs, the operation will wait 10 seconds, then it will proceed to suspend the app. This way, in case the user changes his or her mind and goes back to the app, it's immediately restored.

After that, the app is effectively suspended; it will be stored in memory (so it will keep using RAM) but it won't be able to perform any other operation and it won't be able to use resources such as CPU, network, etc. This way, the new app opened by the user will have the chance to make use of all the device's resources.

As for every other app's life cycle event, the Suspending one is also managed in the **App** class by using the **OnSuspending()** method which, by default, has the following definition:

```
private void OnSuspending(object sender, SuspendingEventArgs e)
{
    var deferral = e.SuspendingOperation.GetDeferral();

    // TODO: Save application state and stop any background activity
    deferral.Complete();
}
```

The main purpose of this method is to allow the developer to save the app's state. Since we can't know if the app will be terminated or not, we need to do it every time the app is suspended.

The previous logic uses the **deferral** concept, which is widely used in Windows Store apps development and needed to manage asynchronous operations. If you recall the basics concepts of the async and await pattern that have been detailed in Chapter 2, when we execute an asynchronous method the compiler sets a sort of bookmark and the method execution is terminated. As a result, the main thread is free to keep managing the UI and the other resources. When we're dealing with the suspending event, this behavior can raise an important issue: the **OnSuspending()** method could be terminated before the operations are completed. The **deferral** object solves this problem; until the **Complete()** method is called, the execution of the **OnSuspending()** method won't terminate.

Of course, to follow the Microsoft guidelines, we can't use this workaround to keep the app running for an indefinite period of time. We have five seconds to save the app's state otherwise the app will be forcedly suspended whether or not the saving operations are completed. As you can see, the timeframe is quite short. As previously mentioned, the purpose of the **OnSuspending()** method is to save the app's state so that the user can't see any difference between a standard suspension and a termination. It's not the ideal place, for instance, to save the app's data.

Resuming

The resume process happens when the app is restored from the suspension but it wasn't terminated by the OS. This process is completely transparent to the developer; since the app was still in memory, the app's state is preserved and we don't need to manually restore it.

However, the **App** class offers a way to intercept this event. Since an app is terminated due to low resources, if the system has enough memory to keep it alive, the app can be suspended for a long time. Consequently, it can happen that, when the app is restored, the data displayed in the page isn't actual anymore.

This is the purpose of the resuming event; it's triggered every time the app is resumed from a suspension without a termination. We can use it to refresh the app's data (for example, by perform a new request to a web service).

By default, the **App** class doesn't manage this event so you'll need to manually subscribe it in the class constructor, like in the following sample:

```
public sealed partial class App : Application
{
    public App()
    {
        this.InitializeComponent();
        this.Resuming += App_Resuming;
    }

    private void App_Resuming(object sender, object e)
    {
        //refresh the data
    }
}
```

Activating

The Windows Runtime offers a contract system, which is used by developers to integrate their apps into the OS. Consequently, a Windows Store app can be launched in different ways than simply by tapping on its tile on the Start screen. It can be triggered by a sharing request or because the user is trying to open a file type which the app is able to manage. In all of these scenarios, the app isn't opened with the launching event but with a specific activation event, which usually contains the required information about the request.

The **App** class offers many activation methods according to the event that triggered the request. For example, the **OnFileActivated()** method is triggered when the app is opened because the user is trying to open a file we support. In Chapter 8, we will take a look at, in detail, all of the available contracts, extensions, and the related activation events.

Closing

The closing event is triggered when the user explicitly closes the app. In Windows 8.1, this operation is performed by dragging the app from the top to the bottom of the screen or by closing the app with a mouse and the close button in the top right corner. In Windows Phone, it's triggered when the user closes it from the Task Switcher, which is activated by pressing a long time on the **Back** button.

However, the closing event on Windows 8.1 doesn't really close the app but, rather, it keeps it in memory so that it can be reopened faster, like with a regular suspension. The only difference is that, this time, the app will start from a `ClosedByUser` state. In this case, we won't have to restore the state since the user has closed the app so he or she expects to start from scratch and not resume a previous usage.

When it comes to Windows Phone, there's an important difference compared to the behavior in Silverlight for Windows Phone 8.0. That is, pressing **Back** on the main page of the app doesn't close it anymore, it just suspends it. The user will always be able to resume the suspended instance no matter how he or she will access the app (from the task switcher, by tapping again on the tile, etc.). In Windows Phone 8.0, this behavior was implemented with a feature called Fast App Resume. In Windows Phone 8.1, this feature is always enabled by default.

Managing the Suspension

In the previous sections of this chapter, we've mentioned the requirement to save the app's state when the app is suspended so that it can be restored in case of termination. Let's take a look, in detail, about how to do it.

Saving the Page's State

The first requirement is to save the current page's state. When the user reopens our app, he or she will expect to return to the last used page in the same state in which he or she left it. When the app is terminated, the page's state is lost. It's our duty to save all the information that we want to maintain. For example, if the current page contains a form that the user is filling out, we need to make sure that, when the app is restored, the previously inserted data will still be there. To support this requirement, Microsoft has created two classes which try to simplify the developer's work. They aren't native Windows Runtime APIs but, instead, they're included in every Windows Store app template offered by Visual Studio (except for the Blank one). It's enough to create a new app by using the Grid App or Hub App template or, alternatively, to add a new page to an existing project by using any page template (except the Blank page one). You'll then find these classes inside a folder called **Common**.

The first class is called `NavigationHelper` and it helps developers to properly manage the navigation between pages. Under the hood, it relies on another class called `SuspensionManager` which is able to automatically save the page's state when the user is moving from one page to another. Let's look at how to use them. The first step is to define a `NavigationHelper` object in the page and to initialize it in the page constructor, like in the following sample:

```
public sealed partial class BasicPage1 : Page
```

```
{
    private NavigationHelper navigationHelper;

    public BasicPage1()
    {
        this.InitializeComponent();

        this.navigationHelper = new NavigationHelper(this);
        this.navigationHelper.LoadState += this.NavigationHelper_LoadState;
        this.navigationHelper.SaveState += this.NavigationHelper_SaveState;
    }

    public NavigationHelper NavigationHelper
    {
        get { return this.navigationHelper; }
    }
}
```

After creating an instance of the **NavigationHelper** class, we subscribe to two events:

- **SaveState** is called when the user moves away from the current page; we're going to use it to save the information we need
- **LoadState** is called when the user is navigating towards the current page; we're going to use it to restore the previously saved information

The last step to properly initialize the **NavigationHelper** is to let it manage the navigation events for us; we're going to override the **OnNavigatedTo()** and **OnNavigatedFrom()** method in the following way:

```
protected override void OnNavigatedTo(NavigationEventArgs e)
{
    this.navigationHelper.OnNavigatedTo(e);
}

protected override void OnNavigatedFrom(NavigationEventArgs e)
{
    this.navigationHelper.OnNavigatedFrom(e);
}
```

Now that the **NavigationHelper** object is properly initialized, we are ready to manage the app's state, thanks to the **SuspensionManager** class. The key feature offered by this class is a collection called **PageState**, which type is **Dictionary<string, object>**: we can store in this collection every information we want to keep, by identifying it with a unique key. Every page will have its unique version of the **PageState** collection.

Let's look at a real example by using an app with a page that contains a **TextBox** control. We want to preserve the text written inside it so that it's not lost (or in case the app is terminated after a suspension). Here is how we can do it, by using the **SaveState** and **LoadState** events offered by the **NavigationHelper** class:

```
private void NavigationHelper_SaveState(object sender, SaveStateEventArgs e)
{
    if (e.PageState != null && e.PageState.ContainsKey("Name"))
    {
        e.PageState.Remove("Name");
    }
    e.PageState.Add("Name", Name.Text);
}


private void NavigationHelper_LoadState(object sender, LoadStateEventArgs e)
{
    if (e.PageState != null && e.PageState.ContainsKey("Name"))
    {
        Name.Text = e.PageState["Name"].ToString();
    }
}
```

In the **SaveState** event's handler, we save the information we want to keep, which is the value of the **Text** property of the **TextBox** control. We perform this operation by adding the text in the **PageState** dictionary and binding it to the **Name** key. First, we check to see whether or not a value with the same key is already there and, in case it is, we remove it. Otherwise, we would get an exception since we can't store two items with the same key in a **Dictionary.**

In the **LoadState** event handler, instead, we retrieve the previously saved information. If inside the **PageState** collection we find an element identified by the **Name** key, we retrieve it and we use it to populate the **TextBox** control.

The work is done: with these simple lines of code, we make sure to properly save the data we need to preserve the page's state.

Saving the App's State

By using the **NavigationHelper** class, we've been able to properly save the page's state thanks to the **PageState** collection. However, the problem is, when the app is suspended and then terminated, the data in memory is lost. When the app is resumed, the different **PageState** collections will be empty. Consequently, we need to save the data in a permanent way so that it can be restored even if the process is terminated and removed from the memory. The best place to store the data is in the local storage, which is the area reserved in the app where data is physically stored so that it can be maintained across different executions. The local storage plays a very important role in app development. We will look in detail in Chapter 5 about how to use it.

For the current scenario, what we need to do is save the **PageState** collections into the local storage and restore them when the app is resumed from a termination. This can be achieved by using the serialization process already mentioned in this book. The content of the various **PageState** collections will be converted into a plain data structure so that it can be saved in the local storage as a text file and vice versa; when the app is resumed, the text file is converted back into objects so that we can restore the original state of the **PageState** collections.

We can use the **SuspensionManager** class to automatically perform this operation for us. The difference with the **NavigationHelper** is that, in this case, the saving and loading operations are connected to the app's life cycle so we need to perform them in the **App** class in which all the life cycle events are managed. The first step is to properly initialize the **SuspensionManager** class, which requires as parameter the root **Frame** of the page. Here is what the **OnLaunched()** method of the App class looks like when you implement the **SuspensionManager**:

```
protected override async void OnLaunched(LaunchActivatedEventArgs e)
{
    Frame rootFrame = Window.Current.Content as Frame;
    if (rootFrame == null)
    {
        rootFrame = new Frame();
        SuspensionManager.RegisterFrame(rootFrame, "AppFrame");
        if (e.PreviousExecutionState == ApplicationExecutionState.Terminated)
        {
            await SuspensionManager.RestoreAsync();
        }
        Window.Current.Content = rootFrame;
    }
    if (rootFrame.Content == null)
    {
        rootFrame.Navigate(typeof (MainPage), e.Arguments);
    }
    Window.Current.Activate();
}
```

We made two important changes to the code we've originally seen for the **OnLaunched()** method:

- Right after creating a new instance of the **Frame** class, we register it to the **SuspensionManager** by calling the **RegisterFrame()** method and passing, as parameter, the **Frame** instance we've just created.
- In case the app comes from a **Terminated** state, we call the **RestoreAsync()** method of the **SuspensionManager**. It will take care of two things; the first one is to fill the **Content** of the **Frame** with the last page visited by the user. Without this operation, the user would be always redirected to the main page. The second one is to re-create all of the **PageState** collection from the data saved in the local storage. This way, every page will have access to the data we've previously saved.

Now that we understand how to restore the state, let's take a look at how to save it. We're going to use the **OnSuspending()** method that is triggered every time the app is suspended:

```
private async void OnSuspending(object sender, SuspendingEventArgs e)
{
    var deferral = e.SuspendingOperation.GetDeferral();
    await SuspensionManager.SaveAsync();
    deferral.Complete();
```

```
}
```

It's not enough to call the `SaveAsync()` method of the `SuspensionManager` class to save, in the storage, the state of the app. It's also important to do it after we've created a deferral object and before calling the `Complete()` method so that the app won't be suspended until all of the data has been properly saved.

Managing Suspension and Resuming Inside a Page

If you have already worked with Windows Phone 8.0 apps based on the Silverlight framework, there's an important difference to keep in mind. In Silverlight, the `OnNavigatedTo()` and `OnNavigatedFrom()` methods are always triggered, not only when the user is navigating from one page to another but also from the page to the Start screen or vice versa. This way, we were able to use these methods to also perform additional operations when the app was suspended or resumed.

The Windows Runtime has changed this behavior. The `OnNavigatedTo()` method won't be triggered anymore when the app will be resumed, while the `OnNavigateFrom()` method won't be triggered when the app will be suspended. If you need to manage this scenario (for example, if you want to refresh the data displayed in the page when the app is resumed), you can subscribe to an event offered by the `Window` class called `VisibilityChanged`. This is triggered when the app is placed in background or vice versa. Let's take a look at an example:

```csharp
public sealed partial class MainPage : Page
{
    public MainPage()
    {
        this.InitializeComponent();
        Window.Current.VisibilityChanged += Current_VisibilityChanged;
    }

    private void Current_VisibilityChanged(object sender,
Windows.UI.Core.VisibilityChangedEventArgs e)
    {
        string message = string.Empty;
        if (e.Visible)
        {
            message = "The application has been activated";
        }
        else
        {
            message = "The application has been suspended";
        }
        Debug.WriteLine(message);
    }
}
```

The `VisibilityChanged` event is offered by the `Windows.Current` object and it offers, as one of the parameters, a property called `Visible`. When it's set to `true`, it means that the app was in background and it's been resumed. When it's set to `false`, we're in the opposite scenario; the app was in the foreground and it's been placed in background because, for example, the user has pressed **Start** or has opened another app.

Testing the App's Life Cycle

Testing all of the scenarios we've described in this chapter could be a challenge as apps aren't terminated following a precise pattern. Rather, it's up to the OS to kill them when resources are low. Consequently, Visual Studio offers a series of options that the developer can use to force the various states of the life cycle. They are available inside a drop-down menu that is included in the **Debug location** toolbar. It's activated once you've launched a debugging session for a Windows Store app:

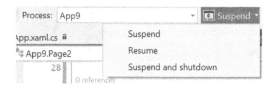

Figure 5: The drop-down menu used to force one of the life cycle's states

The standard available options are:

- **Suspend:** the app is suspended and kept in memory
- **Resume:** the app is resumed from a suspension
- **Suspend and terminate:** it suspends the app and simulates the termination by the OS; this is the option we need to choose if we want to test that we're properly managing the app's state

However, as we're going to see in Chapter 11, this drop-down menu can display additional options since it also helps to test background tasks.

Another scenario that can be hard to test is when the app is activated using a path different from the standard launching event (such as a secondary tile, a notification, or a contract). To help the developers testing these cases, Visual Studio offers an option that allows the debugger to start (but without effectively launching) the app. This way, no matter which way is used to activate the app, the debugger will be connected and ready to catch any error or to help in debugging specific issues. This option can be enabled in the project's properties (you can see them by right-clicking the project in Solution Explorer and choosing Properties). You can find it in the **Debug** section entitled "Do not launch, but debug my code when it starts":

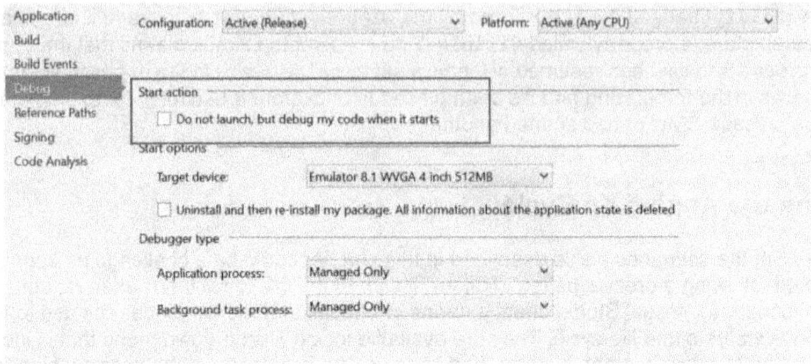

Figure 6: The option to enable the debugging of the app (without launching it)

Chapter 5 Working with Files: Storage, Database, and Settings

The Storage

Windows Store apps' storage management is another big difference compared to the traditional Windows apps approach. If desktop apps are able to virtually write and read files in any computer's folder, Windows Store apps run in a sandbox. The storage works like a standard hard drive but it's isolated: apps can't read and write data outside this sandbox (unless the user explicitly allows it). The most important advantage of this approach is security. Apps aren't able to access the core OS's files so they can't corrupt the phone's integrity, whether intentionally or by mistake due to a bug. The data saved in the local storage is persisted; even if the app is closed or suspended, the data is not lost but, rather, is always available every time it's launched again.

The Windows Runtime offers different types of storage which are available thanks to the `ApplicationData.Current` class that is part of the `Windows.Storage` namespace. Let's take a look, in detail, at the available storages.

The Local Storage

The local storage is identified by the `LocalFolder` class and it's the most widely used. It's a traditional file system in which you can create files and folders just as you do on your computer's hard disk. However, due to the isolated nature of the storage, the stored data can be accessed only by your app. Other apps can access to your data only by using a special contract (which will be detailed in Chapter 8).

The local storage follows the same life cycle of the app: once it's uninstalled, the storage is also removed. There are no limitations in the storage quota that an app can use, other than the free available space on the device. The local storage also offers an easy way to manage a common scenario in app development (which is storing and reading settings) thanks to a class called `LocalSettings`. We'll look at how to use it in more detail later in this chapter.

One important thing to mention about the local storage is that it's strictly connected to the new backup feature introduced in Windows Phone 8.1. In fact, in the latest Windows Phone version, the built-in backup feature is able to save more than just the phone's settings, including such things as the Start screen configuration, the e-mail accounts, or the lock screen image (also the local storage's content of 8.1 apps). This way, if the user resets his or her phone or buys a new one, he or she will find it in its exact previous state, including its app's data.

It's important to highlight that this backup is saved to OneDrive (even if it's transparent to the user, he or she won't be able to see the data on his or her account) and it counts against his or her quota.

The Local Storage without Backup Support (Windows Phone Only)

The automatic backup feature applied to the local storage is helpful because, as developers, we don't have to find an alternative way to provide a backup mechanism for our app. However, there are some apps that don't play well with this feature. If the app downloads a lot of data from the Internet, it could be a waste of the OneDrive user's storage, saving everything on the cloud.

For example, think about an app such as Spotify or Xbox Music. The local storage can become quite big since the user has the ability to download the music offline so that they can listen to it without an Internet connection. In this case, we're not talking about content generated by the user but, rather, about content that is simply downloaded from Internet and stored locally.

For all of these scenarios, where saving the whole app's content would be a waste of space on the user's OneDrive account, Windows Phone 8.1 provides a special storage called `LocalCacheFolder` which is also part of the `ApplicationData.Current` class. It works exactly like the `LocalFolder`; the only difference is that the data created and put into this storage is not automatically saved during the backup procedure.

The Roaming Storage

The roaming storage is identified by the `RoamingStorage` class offered, as usual, by the `ApplicationData.Current` object. It has the same basic features of the local storage, which means that the data is isolated and it can store settings (by using the `RoamingSettings` class), files, and folders.

The most important feature of the roaming storage is that the data is automatically synchronized with all the devices of the users that are registered under the same Microsoft Account, whether or not they are Windows 8.1 computers, Windows 8.1 tablets, or Windows Phone 8.1 smartphones. This means that, if the user has installed the same app on multiple devices, we are able to synchronize the data so that, for example, the user can start a job on the tablet and then resume it on the phone (or the user can find the same settings on the phone that he or she configured on his or her tablet).

The roaming's storage doesn't follow the same life cycle of the app. Even if it's uninstalled, the roaming data is kept for 30 days in case the user changes his or her mind and decides to reinstall the app again. The roaming storage is based on OneDrive, even if it doesn't count against the user's quota. However, there's an important limitation when it comes to the storage's size. The current limit is, in fact, 100 KB. Consequently, the roaming storage is ideal to save small data such as the app's settings and not the real content (such as a database). If you need to synchronize the app's content, it's better to rely on a third-party solution (such as the mobile services offered by Azure, Microsoft's cloud solution).

However, the 100KB limit is not fixed as Microsoft could decide to increase it in the future. For this reason, when you need to save some data in the roaming storage and you want to make sure to fill the maximum space, you don't have to check against the 100KB quota but against a special property called `RoamingStorageQuota`. In this case, if Microsoft decides to increase it in a future Windows update, you won't have to change your code to support the new quota. The following sample shows how to retrieve this information so that we can display it to the user with a pop-up message:

```csharp
private async void OnShowQuotaClicked(object sender, RoutedEventArgs e)
{
    string quota = string.Format("Roaming quota: {0} KB",
ApplicationData.Current.RoamingStorageQuota);
    MessageDialog dialog = new MessageDialog(quota);
    await dialog.ShowAsync();
}
```

What happens if you exceed the roaming quota? Nothing, as the data simply won't be synchronized anymore until you delete some content. Another important limitation to mention is that the synchronization isn't performed instantly but, rather, it depends on many scenarios including the network availability, whether or not the device is running in battery saver mode, etc. Consequently, you shouldn't rely on the roaming storage for critical scenarios in which you need the data to be synchronized as soon as possible on all the devices.

Since the synchronization is performed out of developer's control, we can subscribe to an event called **DataChanged** (offered by the **ApplicationData.Current** class) which is triggered when the synchronization has been performed and the data has been updated. This way, if for example the settings are changed, we can perform the required operations to properly update the app's behavior. The following sample shows how to subscribe to this event:

```csharp
public sealed partial class MainPage : Page
{
    public MainPage()
    {
        this.InitializeComponent();
        ApplicationData.Current.DataChanged += Current_DataChanged;
    }

    private void Current_DataChanged(ApplicationData sender, object args)
    {
        //update the application
    }
}
```

The Temporary Storage

The last storage's type is called temporary storage and it is identified by the **TemporaryFolder** class offered by the **ApplicationData.Current** object. It's used mainly for caching scenarios, which means data that can be useful to speed up the app (such as keeping a set of images downloaded from Internet) but that aren't critical. This storage, in fact, can be erased at any time, without notice, by the user (in case he or she decides to clean up the temporary files) or by the system (in case of a maintenance task).

Unlike the other two storage's types, the temporary storage doesn't support settings management.

Working with Folders

A common scenario for developers is to organize the storage's structure by using folders in order to keep files separated in a logical way. Every folder in the Windows Runtime is identified by the **StorageFolder** class which offers many methods to perform the most common operations (such as creating a new file, getting the list of available files, renaming a file, etc.).

Consequently, the main root of every storage's type (for example, the **LocalFolder** and the **RoamingFolder** objects) are identified with the **StorageFolder** class. Here is a brief list of the most common operations that can be performed:

- **CreateFolderAsync()** to create a new folder
- **GetFolderAsync()** to get a reference to an existing subfolder
- **DeleteAsync()** to delete a folder
- **RenameAsync()** to rename a folder

The following sample code shows how to create a folder inside the local storage:

```
private async void OnCreateFolderClicked(object sender, RoutedEventArgs e)
{
    await ApplicationData.Current.LocalFolder.CreateFolderAsync("myFolder");
    await
ApplicationData.Current.LocalFolder.CreateFolderAsync("myFolder2\\mySubFolder");
}
```

As you can see, you're able to manipulate not just folders but also subfolders by using the backslash (\) as separator between one folder and the other. If one of the subfolders doesn't exist, the Windows Runtime will create it (for example, the second line of code will create both the myFolder2 and mySubFolder folders). In this case, we're using a double backslash just to properly escape this special character.

The Windows Runtime also offers a way to check to see if a folder already exists before performing any operation by using the **TryGetItemAsync()** method. If the folder exists, you will get a reference to it in return; if not, you'll get a **null** object. The following code, before creating a new folder called myFolder, checks to see if it already exists in the local storage:

```
private async void OnCreateFolderClicked(object sender, RoutedEventArgs e)
{
    IStorageItem storageItem = await ApplicationData.Current.LocalFolder.
TryGetItemAsync("myFolder");
    if (storageItem == null)
    {
        await ApplicationData.Current.LocalFolder.CreateFolderAsync("myFolder");
    }
}
```

 Note: The TryGetItemAsync() method is available only in Windows. In Windows Phone, the only way to check to see if a folder exists is to use

the GetFolderAsync() method and, by using a try / catch statement, catch the exception that is raised in case the folder doesn't exist.

Working with Files

Files are identified by the **StorageFile** class which offers a set of methods to perform the most common operations such as:

- **DeleteAsync()** to delete a file
- **RenameAsync()** to rename a file
- **CopyAsync()** to copy a file from one location to another
- **MoveAsync()** to move a file from one location to another

The starting point from which to work with a file is the **StorageFolder** class since each file belongs to a folder (since, as we've mentioned, the storage's root is also treated as a folder). We have two different options: to create a new file by using the **CreateFileAsync()** method or to get a reference to an existing file by using the **GetFileAsync()** method.

Let's look at how to write and read a file in the local storage. The Windows Runtime offers two different approaches, one based on streams and the other on bulk operations.

Creating and Reading a File as a Stream

To create a file, we need to use the **CreateFileAsync()** method offered by the **StorageFolder** class which accepts as parameter the file's name. The following sample shows how to create a text file in the local storage:

```
private async void OnCreateFileClicked(object sender, RoutedEventArgs e)
{
    StorageFile file = await
ApplicationData.Current.LocalFolder.CreateFileAsync("file.txt");
}
```

In return, you'll get a reference to the file you've just created. Also, when you're working with files, you can use the **TryGetItemAsync()** method we've previously seen with folders to check to see whether or not a file already exists before performing any operation, like in the following sample:

```
private async void OnCreateFileClicked(object sender, RoutedEventArgs e)
{
    IStorageItem storageItem = await
ApplicationData.Current.LocalFolder.TryGetItemAsync("file.txt");
    if (storageItem == null)
    {
        StorageFile file = await
ApplicationData.Current.LocalFolder.CreateFileAsync("file.txt");
    }
```

```
}
```

Once you have a reference to the file, you can call the **OpenAsync()** method to get the reading or writing stream. The type of stream is defined by the **FileAccessMode** property which is passed as parameter. To perform a writing operation, we need to use the **ReadWrite** value, like in the following sample:

```
private async void OnCreateFileClicked(object sender, RoutedEventArgs e)
{
    IStorageItem storageItem = await
ApplicationData.Current.LocalFolder.TryGetItemAsync("file.txt");
    if (storageItem == null)
    {
        StorageFile file = await
ApplicationData.Current.LocalFolder.CreateFileAsync("file.txt");
        IRandomAccessStream randomAccessStream = await
file.OpenAsync(FileAccessMode.ReadWrite);
        using (DataWriter writer = new
DataWriter(randomAccessStream.GetOutputStreamAt(0)))
        {
            writer.WriteString("Sample text");
            await writer.StoreAsync();
        }
    }
}
```

When you open the file by using the **OpenAsync()** method, you get a reference to the content's stream which is identified by the **IRandomAccessStream** class. Thanks to this stream, you'll be able to use the **DataWriter** class to perform writing operations. It's important to highlight that the **IRandomAccessStream** class provides access both to a writing and a reading stream. In this case, since we want to write some content to the file, we need to the use the output stream, which is obtained using the **GetOutputStreamAt()** method. The parameter identifies the stream position from which we want to start the writing operation. In our case, we use **0** to start from the beginning.

The **DataWriter** class is a special Windows Runtime class that makes it easier to write the most common data types to a file. In the sample, you can see the **WriteString()** method to write a text but you can use also, for example, **WriteBytes()** to write binary content, **WriteDouble()** to write a number, **WriteDateTime()** to write a date, and so on. Once you've written the content to the file, you can finalize the operation by calling the **StoreAsync()** method.

The approach to read the file's content is a similar one. Also in this case, after getting a reference to the file by using the **GetFileAsync()** method, we need to open it by using the **OpenAsync()** method. In this case, since we just need to read the content, we can pass as parameter the **Read** value of the **FileAccessMode** enumerator. Here is a full sample:

```
private async void OnReadFileClicked(object sender, RoutedEventArgs e)
{
    IStorageItem storageItem = await
ApplicationData.Current.LocalFolder.TryGetItemAsync("file.txt");
    if (storageItem != null)
    {
        StorageFile file = await
        ApplicationData.Current.LocalFolder.GetFileAsync("file.txt");
        IRandomAccessStream randomAccessStream = await
        file.OpenAsync(FileAccessMode.Read);
        using (DataReader reader = new
        DataReader(randomAccessStream.GetInputStreamAt(0)))
        {
            uint bytesLoaded = await reader.LoadAsync((uint)randomAccessStream.Size);
            string readString = reader.ReadString(bytesLoaded);
            MessageDialog dialog = new MessageDialog(readString);
            await dialog.ShowAsync();
        }
    }
}
```

As you can see, the code is very similar to the standard procedure. The main differences are:

- Since, in this case, we want to perform a reading operation, we need to retrieve the input stream by using the **GetInputStreamAt()** method offered by the **IRandomAccessStream** class. Also in this case, we need to specify the stream's position from which to start the reading operation. By using **0**, we're going to read the content from the beginning.
- Instead of the **DataWriter** class, we used the **DataReader** one, which works in the same way. It offers a set of methods to read the most common data types. In this case, since we're reading a text file, we call the **ReadString()** method but we could have used **ReadDouble()** to read a number or **ReadDateTime()** to read a date.

Creating and Reading a File with a Bulk Operation

In the previous section, we saw that, thanks to the **DataWriter** and **DataReader** classes, we are able work with files as streams. We are able to start the writing or reading procedure from any position and not just from the beginning. However, this precision isn't always required. For these scenarios, the Windows Runtime offers a class called **FileIO** (which is part of the **Windows.Storage** namespace), which is easier to use to perform basic read and write operations.

The starting point is, as usual, the **StorageFile** class so we still need to use the APIs we've previously seen to create a file (in case of a writing procedure) or to get a reference to an existing one (in case of a reading procedure). The methods exposed by the **FileIO** class offers a simple way to write the most common data types such as **WriteTextAsync()** to write a string or **WriteBufferAsync()** to write a binary content such as an image. The following sample shows how to create a text file in the local storage:

```
private async void OnCreateFileClicked(object sender, RoutedEventArgs e)
{
    StorageFile file = await
ApplicationData.Current.LocalFolder.CreateFileAsync("file.txt");
    await FileIO.WriteTextAsync(file, "Sample text");
}
```

You can also add a text to an existing file by using the **AppendTextAsync()** method:

```
private async void OnReadFileClicked(object sender, RoutedEventArgs e)
{
    StorageFile file = await
ApplicationData.Current.LocalFolder.GetFileAsync("file.txt");
    await FileIO.AppendTextAsync(file, "Sample text to append");
}
```

The reading operations are performed in the same way, by using the reading methods offered by the **FileIO** class (such as **ReadTextAsync()** to read a string or **ReadBufferAsync()** to read a binary file). The following sample shows how to retrieve the previously saved text:

```
private async void OnReadFileClicked(object sender, RoutedEventArgs e)
{
    StorageFile file = await
ApplicationData.Current.LocalFolder.GetFileAsync("file.txt");
    string text = await FileIO.ReadTextAsync(file);
}
```

Accessing Files by Using URLs

In some scenarios, it can be useful to access the app's files by using an URL. For example, this can be the case when you're using an **Image** control and you want to display an image that's stored in the local storage. In Windows Store apps, you can use some special protocols to get access to the files of your app:

- The **ms-appx:///** protocol is used to provide access to the files that are part of the Visual Studio project. However, to access to these files, you need to make sure that the **Build action** property (which can be set by right-clicking the file in Visual Studio and choosing **Properties**) is set to **Content**. For example, let's say that you have an image called **logo.png** placed in the Assets folder of your project. The following sample shows how to display it by using an **Image** control in the XAML:

```
<Image Source="ms-appx:///Assets/logo.png" />
```

- The `ms-appdata:///` protocol is used to provide access to the files that are stored in one of the available storage's types. After the protocol, you need to specify which storage you want to use: `local`, `localcache`, `roaming` or `temporary`. The following sample shows how to use an `Image` control to display an image stored in the local storage:

```
<Image Source="ms-appdata:///local/Assets/logo.png" />
```

Debugging the App: Checking the Storage's Content

When you're developing and testing an app that writes some data to the storage, it is important to verify that everything is working fine and that the files are effectively created in the storage. Let's look at how to do this.

Checking the Storage's Content in Windows

The local storage in Windows is stored inside a special folder in the path *%USERPROFILE%\AppData\Local\Packages* (%USERPROFILE% is a special string that represents the root folder of your user account). Inside this folder, you'll find many subfolders; each of them identifies one of the Windows Store apps you've installed on your device. Typically, apps manually deployed from Visual Studio and not installed from the Store are identified by the Package Name, which is an identifier that you can find in the Packaging section of the manifest file.

Inside this folder, you'll find some subfolders; each of them refers to one of the storage's types. You'll simply have to open the folder which you're interested in and verify that the data inside it is correct.

Checking the Storage's Content in Windows Phone

Checking the storage's content in Windows Phone isn't as easy as it is in Windows since the platform allows users and developers to explore just some of the phone's libraries (such as pictures, videos, documents, etc.). You can't access the OS's folders or the location to which local storage is saved. Visual Studio 2013 includes a tool to explore the phone's storage but it's not very intuitive to use since it's a command-line app.

Consequently, many developers have created third-party tools that, by relying on this app, offer a visual interface which is easier for developers to use. One of the best available tools is called **Windows Phone Power Tools** and can be downloaded here.

Using this tool is easy. When you start it, a drop-down menu will allow you to choose between the device and one of the available emulators. Once the connection is successful, you'll be able to use the Isolated Storage section to see the apps that have been manually deployed on the phone (by using Visual Studio or the app deployment tool provided with the SDK). Of course, for security reasons, you won't be able to explore the local storage of apps installed from the Store.

Once you've chosen the right app, you'll be able to perform the most common operations like you can do with a regular file explorer. You can browse, open, delete, or download files, or even upload a file from your computer to the phone (which can be useful to simulate real data during the testing phase).

Managing the App's Settings

A common consideration while developing an app is settings management; the app can offer a settings page where the user can customize the app according to their needs. Both the local storage and the roaming storage offer an easy way to manage this scenario, by offering a class (**LocalSettings** for local storage, **RoamingSettings** for roaming storage) which is a collection where we can save our settings and identify them with a unique key so that we can retrieve them later.

Under the hood, it works in a similar fashion as the feature we described in Chapter 4 regarding managing the page's state. The settings are identified with a **Dictionary<string, object>** collection where we can save our data (which can be a generic object), each of them identified by a string key. This data is automatically serialized and deserialized when it's needed so that it's persisted and maintained even if the app is closed.

The dictionary is stored in the **Value** property offered by the **LocalSettings** and the **RoamingSettings** classes. The following sample shows how to save some data into the roaming settings:

```
private void OnSaveSettingsClicked(object sender, RoutedEventArgs e)
{
    if (ApplicationData.Current.RoamingSettings.Values.ContainsKey("IsEnabled"))
    {
        ApplicationData.Current.RoamingSettings.Values.Remove("IsEnabled");
    }
    ApplicationData.Current.RoamingSettings.Values.Add("IsEnabled", true);
}
```

First we check, by using the **ContainsKey()** method, whether or not a value associated with a specific key already exists (in the sample, it's called **IsEnabled**). If it does, before saving it using the **Add()** method, we delete it from the collection by using the **Remove()** method.

The following sample shows how to retrieve the recently saved value from the roaming settings:

```
private async void OnReadSettingsClicked(object sender, RoutedEventArgs e)
{
    if (ApplicationData.Current.LocalSettings.Values.ContainsKey("IsEnabled"))
    {
        bool isEnabled =
(bool)ApplicationData.Current.LocalSettings.Values["IsEnabled"];
        MessageDialog dialog = new MessageDialog(isEnabled.ToString());
        await dialog.ShowAsync();
    }
```

```
}
```

The syntax should be familiar since it's the standard one used when you work with **Dictionary** collections. After checking to see whether or not the value identified by the **IsEnabled** key exists, we retrieve it by specifying the key's name inside square brackets. Since the dictionary can store a generic object, we need to perform a cast to the object's type we expect. In our case, we cast it to **bool** since we previously saved a **Boolean** value.

It's important to highlight that the settings aren't able to store any type of data but only the native Windows Runtime types, which are listed in official MSDN documentation here.

When it comes to managing settings, the best storage type to use is the roaming one. This way, if you're working on a Universal Windows app that can be installed both on Windows and on Windows Phone, you'll be able to share the settings across the two different versions so that the user won't have to customize the app twice.

Organizing Settings

The settings classes we've previously discussed also offer an easy way to organize the settings in different containers that, for example, can be related to different sections of your app. This way, instead of having all of the settings stored in just one collection, you can split them into many dictionaries, each of them with its own unique identifier.

To use containers, you first have to call the **CreateContainer()** method offered by one of the settings classes. The required parameters are the container's name and a value of the **ApplicationDataCreateDisposition** enumerator which tells the Windows Runtime if the container should be created (if it doesn't exist). Once you've created the container, it works like the standard settings; you'll have access to a property called **Values** which is a **Dictionary<string, object>** collection. The following sample shows how to create a collection with name **MainSettings** in which we save an integer value:

```
private void OnSaveSettingsClicked(object sender, RoutedEventArgs e)
{
    ApplicationDataContainer container = ApplicationData.Current.LocalSettings.
    CreateContainer("MainSettings", ApplicationDataCreateDisposition.Always);
    container.Values.Add("NumberOfItems", 10);
}
```

To get access to the existing containers, you can use the **Containers** property offered by the **LocalSettings** and **RoamingSettings** classes, which is a collection of all the available containers. Once you've retrieved a reference to the desired container, you can again use the **Values** collection to get the setting you're looking for, in the same way we previously did:

```
private async void OnReadSettingsClicked(object sender, RoutedEventArgs e)
{
    if (ApplicationData.Current.LocalSettings.Containers.ContainsKey("MainSettings"))
    {
        ApplicationDataContainer container =
ApplicationData.Current.LocalSettings.Containers["MainSettings"];
```

```
        int numberOfItems = (int)container.Values["NumberOfItems"];
        MessageDialog dialog = new MessageDialog(numberOfItems.ToString());
        await dialog.ShowAsync();
    }
}
```

Integrating Settings in a Windows App

So far, we've seen how to manage settings from a logical point of view. **LocalSettings** and **RoamingSettings** are two classes that make it easier for the developer to store and read data. Now let's take a look at how to integrate settings in our app from a visual point of view. Windows Phone doesn't have any specific requirement. Typically, you just define a new page in the app and you provide in the main page a quick way for the user to access it.

In Windows 8.1, you have a specific requirement which is connected to the Charms bar. If you open the Charms Bar (the one on the right side of the screen), you'll find a button called **Settings**. When you press **Settings**, a panel from the right is opened; this is the place to include all of the app's settings:

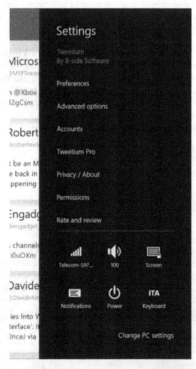

Figure 7: The Settings panel of a Windows Store app for Windows

Let's take a look at how to include our settings into this panel. The first step is to create the layout in which to place our settings. Each section is identified by a page which works like a traditional one. The only difference is that, instead of being displayed in full screen, it's placed inside the right panel. Consequently, we need to keep in mind that we have less space to include our XAML controls.

To help developers, Visual Studio includes a specific template for settings pages. You can find it by right-clicking your project in Solution Explorer and choosing **Add new item**. You'll find an option called **Settings Flyout**. This template will add a XAML control that, instead of inheriting from the **Page** class, it will derive from the **SettingsFlyout** one.

Here is a sample definition:

```
<SettingsFlyout
    x:Class="SampleApp.SettingsFlyout1"
    xmlns="http://schemas.microsoft.com/winfx/2006/xaml/presentation"
    xmlns:x="http://schemas.microsoft.com/winfx/2006/xaml"
    xmlns:d="http://schemas.microsoft.com/expression/blend/2008"
    xmlns:mc="http://schemas.openxmlformats.org/markup-compatibility/2006"
    mc:Ignorable="d"
    IconSource="Assets/SmallLogo.png"
    Title="SettingsFlyout1"
    d:DesignWidth="346">

    <StackPanel VerticalAlignment="Stretch" HorizontalAlignment="Stretch" >

        <StackPanel VerticalAlignment="Stretch" HorizontalAlignment="Stretch" >
            <StackPanel Style="{StaticResource SettingsFlyoutSectionStyle}">
                <TextBlock Style="{StaticResource TitleTextBlockStyle}" Text="Setup
transfers" />
                <ToggleSwitch Header="Enable download" />
                <ToggleSwitch Header="Enable upload" />
            </StackPanel>
        </StackPanel>

    </StackPanel>
</SettingsFlyout>
```

The main differences, compared to a standard page, can be found in some of the properties of the **SettingsFlyout** class:

- It has a width of 346 pixels, which is the size of the Settings panel
- It has a title, which is set by the **Title** property
- It has an icon that is displayed near the title, which is set by the **IconSource** property

Except for these differences, the **SettingsFlyout** works just like a regular page. You can place any XAML control inside it (in the sample, we've added a **TextBlock** as header and two **ToggleSwitch** buttons) and, in the code behind, you can define the logic to store the values in the settings by using the approach we've seen previously in this chapter.

What we need to properly manage is the integration with the Charm bar. When the Settings button is pressed and our app is opened, we need to display the list of settings and the pages we've created. To do this, we need to use the OnWindowCreated() method which is offered by the App class. This method is triggered when the app's window is created:

```
protected override void OnWindowCreated(WindowCreatedEventArgs args)
{
    SettingsPane.GetForCurrentView().CommandsRequested += App_CommandsRequested;
}

private void App_CommandsRequested(SettingsPane sender,
SettingsPaneCommandsRequestedEventArgs args)
{
    //manage the settings
}
```

After we've retrieved a reference to the settings panel of the current app (by calling the GetForCurrentView() method of the SettingsPane class), we subscribe to the CommandsRequested event which is invoked when the user presses **Settings**.

When you press **Settings**, you'll see a list of options which represents the different sections used to organize the settings. What we need to do in this event handler is to load all the sections which are simply a shortcut to the different settings pages we've previously created:

```
private void App_CommandsRequested(SettingsPane sender,
SettingsPaneCommandsRequestedEventArgs args)
{
    SettingsCommand command = new SettingsCommand("Settings", "Settings", handler
=>
    {
        SettingsFlyout1 settings = new SettingsFlyout1();
        settings.Show();
    });
    args.Request.ApplicationCommands.Add(command);
}
```

We can have as many settings pages as we want; we just have to register all of them in the CommandsRequested event handler like in the previous sample. In this case, we have just one setting page which is represented by the XAML page we previously created. Every section is identified by a SettingsCommand which requires as parameters:

- A unique identifier of the command
- The name of the section that will be displayed in the Settings panel
- The operations to perform when the user taps on the section's name in the panel

Typically, when the user taps on the section name, we need to display the settings page we've defined. We can do this by creating a new instance of the SettingsFlyout page we've previously created and then calling the Show() method.

The last step is to add all the `SettingsCommand` we've defined to the list of available sections that are displayed when the user taps on **Settings** in the Charms Bar. This list is represented by the `ApplicationCommands` collection which is one of the properties exposed by the method's parameter. We simply call the `Add()` method, passing as parameter the `SettingsCommand` object we've defined.

Accessing the Files that are Included in the Project

When you download an app from the Store, the OS unpacks the package created by Visual Studio in a special system folder, which developers and users can't access. Typically, the content of this folder matches the structure of your project in Visual Studio. Consequently, you may be required to access one of these files (such as a database or an image) from the code while the app is running. You can do this by using a special class called `Package.Current.InstalledLocation` which identifies your project's root. It behaves like regular storage; every folder (including the `InstalledLocation` object itself) is identified with the `StorageFolder` class while files are mapped with the `StorageFile` class.

The only important difference between this and the local storage is that you can't write data in the app folder, you can only read them. Every method to perform writing operations (such as `CreateFileAsync()`) will throw an exception. The following sample shows how to get a reference to a file stored in the project and to copy it to the local storage:

```
private async void OnCopyFileClicked(object sender, RoutedEventArgs e)
{
    StorageFile file = await
Package.Current.InstalledLocation.GetFileAsync("file.xml");
    await file.CopyAsync(ApplicationData.Current.LocalFolder);
}
```

Importing a File or a Folder Stored in the Device

In this chapter, we've learned that the local storage is isolated; we can't directly access the data created by other apps or stored in the phone (such as documents, images, or music tracks). Since this approach can become a serious limitation for many apps, the Windows Runtime offers a class called `FileOpenPicker` that can be used to import external files into our app. The `FileOpenPicker` class opens a special dialog box that is managed by the OS and that can be used to browse the various device's folders.

Since Windows supports the ability to run multiple apps at the same time, while Windows Phone doesn't, the implementation of this class is different based on the platform. Let's look in detail about how to use it on both platforms.

Importing a File or a Folder in Windows

The way to use the `FileOpenPicker` class to import a file in Windows is simple, as you can see in the following sample:

```
private async void OnPickFileClicked(object sender, RoutedEventArgs e)
{
    FileOpenPicker picker = new FileOpenPicker();
    picker.FileTypeFilter.Add(".jpg");
    picker.FileTypeFilter.Add(".png");
    StorageFile file = await picker.PickSingleFileAsync();
    if (file != null)
    {
        await file.CopyAsync(ApplicationData.Current.LocalFolder);
    }
}
```

The first option to set is the kind of files we want to import. This way, the picker will automatically display only the files that match the extension we choose. We need to add at least one extension to the **FileTypeFilter** collection, otherwise we'll get an exception. If we want to support any kind of file, we can just add the asterisk (*) as the file's type.

Once you've defined the supported extension, you just need to call the **PickSingleFileAsync()** method. The picker's UI will be opened and the user will be able to choose any of the files on the device. Once they have made their choice, the picker will be closed and the control will be returned to your app. The **PickSingleFileAsync()** method will return a **StorageFile** object which contains the file selected by the user. The previous sample shows how to copy this file into the local storage. It's important to always check that the file is not **null** before performing any operation since the user has the chance to cancel the import operation.

You can also use the **FileOpenPicker** class to import multiple files with a single operation by calling the **PickMultipleFileAsync()**. It works in the same way as the previous way, with the only difference being, instead of returning a single **StorageFile** object, it returns a collection of them. The following sample shows how to copy all the selected files into the local storage of the app:

```
private async void OnPickFilesClicked(object sender, RoutedEventArgs e)
{
    FileOpenPicker picker = new FileOpenPicker();
    picker.FileTypeFilter.Add(".png");
    IReadOnlyList<StorageFile> files = await picker.PickMultipleFilesAsync();
    if (files.Count > 0)
    {
        foreach (StorageFile file in files)
        {
            await file.CopyAsync(ApplicationData.Current.LocalFolder);
        }
    }
}
```

Files aren't the only thing that can be imported. You can also import an entire folder, which means that you'll get access to all of the files that are included in the folder. The operation is achieved in a similar way, with the exception that, in this case, we're using the **FolderPicker** class, like in the following sample:

```
private async void OnPickFolderClicked(object sender, RoutedEventArgs e)
{
    FolderPicker picker = new FolderPicker();
    picker.FileTypeFilter.Add("*");
    StorageFolder folder = await picker.PickSingleFolderAsync();
    if (folder != null)
    {
        var files = await folder.GetFilesAsync();
        foreach (StorageFile file in files)
        {
            MessageDialog dialog = new MessageDialog(file.DisplayName);
            await dialog.ShowAsync();
        }
    }
}
```

Also, in this case, we need to add at least one element to the **FileTypeFilter** collection but, since folders don't have a type, it's enough to pass an asterisk (*) so that the user can import any folder on the device. Then, you can call the **PickSingleFolderAsync()** method which will open the usual picker UI. Once the user has selected a folder, the method will return a **StorageFolder** object that references it. This way, you'll be able to perform additional operations on the folder such as creating, opening, or deleting a file, or creating a subfolder, etc. The previous sample gets the list of all of the files included in the folder and shows their name via a pop-up message.

Importing a File or a Folder in Windows Phone

Since Windows Phone isn't able to keep two apps opened at the same time, when you activate the **FileOpenPicker**, the current app is suspended (to be resumed after the user has chosen the file or the folder to import). Consequently, after we've configured the **FileOpenPicker** in the same way as we did in Windows, we need to use methods that are available only on Windows Phone to activate it. These are called **PickSingleFileAndContinue()** for importing a single file and **PickMultipleFilesAndContinue()** for importing multiple files.

Here is a complete sample:

```
private void OnOpenFileClicked(object sender, RoutedEventArgs e)
{
    FileOpenPicker picker = new FileOpenPicker();
    picker.FileTypeFilter.Add(".jpg");
    picker.FileTypeFilter.Add(".png");
    picker.PickSingleFileAndContinue();
}
```

As you can see, the biggest difference with the Windows approach is that the **PickSingleFileAndContinue()** method doesn't return a reference to the selected file; we need to get it in another way since the app is suspended.

To help developers to manage this scenario, Microsoft has created a class called **ContinuationManager**; however, it's not included in the Windows Runtime. Instead, Microsoft has published the source code in the MSDN documentation. Here is the full class definition which you can copy into a new class inside your project:

```
#if WINDOWS_PHONE_APP
    /// <summary>
    /// ContinuationManager is used to detect if the most recent activation was due
    /// to a continuation such as the FileOpenPicker or WebAuthenticationBroker
    /// </summary>
    public class ContinuationManager
    {
        IContinuationActivatedEventArgs args = null;
        bool handled = false;
        Guid id = Guid.Empty;

        /// <summary>
        /// Sets the ContinuationArgs for this instance using default frame of
current Window
        /// Should be called by the main activation handling code in App.xaml.cs
        /// </summary>
        /// <param name="args">The activation args</param>
        internal void Continue(IContinuationActivatedEventArgs args)
        {
            Continue(args, Window.Current.Content as Frame);
        }

        /// <summary>
        /// Sets the ContinuationArgs for this instance. Should be called by the
main activation
        /// handling code in App.xaml.cs
        /// </summary>
        /// <param name="args">The activation args</param>
        /// <param name="rootFrame">The frame control that contains the current
page</param>
        internal void Continue(IContinuationActivatedEventArgs args, Frame
rootFrame)
        {
            if (args == null)
                throw new ArgumentNullException("args");

            if (this.args != null && !handled)
                throw new InvalidOperationException("Can't set args more than
once");

            this.args = args;
            this.handled = false;
            this.id = Guid.NewGuid();

            if (rootFrame == null)
```

```csharp
                    return;

                switch (args.Kind)
                {
                    case ActivationKind.PickFileContinuation:
                        var fileOpenPickerPage = rootFrame.Content as
IFileOpenPickerContinuable;
                        if (fileOpenPickerPage != null)
                        {
                            fileOpenPickerPage.ContinueFileOpenPicker(args as
FileOpenPickerContinuationEventArgs);
                        }
                        break;

                    case ActivationKind.PickSaveFileContinuation:
                        var fileSavePickerPage = rootFrame.Content as
IFileSavePickerContinuable;
                        if (fileSavePickerPage != null)
                        {
                            fileSavePickerPage.ContinueFileSavePicker(args as
FileSavePickerContinuationEventArgs);
                        }
                        break;

                    case ActivationKind.PickFolderContinuation:
                        var folderPickerPage = rootFrame.Content as
IFolderPickerContinuable;
                        if (folderPickerPage != null)
                        {
                            folderPickerPage.ContinueFolderPicker(args as
FolderPickerContinuationEventArgs);
                        }
                        break;

                    case ActivationKind.WebAuthenticationBrokerContinuation:
                        var wabPage = rootFrame.Content as
IWebAuthenticationContinuable;
                        if (wabPage != null)
                        {
                            wabPage.ContinueWebAuthentication(args as
WebAuthenticationBrokerContinuationEventArgs);
                        }
                        break;
                }
        }

        /// <summary>
        /// Marks the contination data as 'stale', meaning that it is probably no
longer useful.
        /// Called when the app is suspended (to ensure future activations don't
appear
        /// to be for the same continuation) and whenever the continuation data is
retrieved
        /// (so that it isn't retrieved on subsequent navigations)
        /// </summary>
```

```csharp
        internal void MarkAsStale()
        {
            this.handled = true;
        }

        /// <summary>
        /// Retrieves the continuation args if they have not already been retrieved
and
        /// prevents further retrieval via this property (to avoid accidental
double usage)
        /// </summary>
        public IContinuationActivatedEventArgs ContinuationArgs
        {
            get
            {
                if (handled)
                    return null;
                MarkAsStale();
                return args;
            }
        }

        /// <summary>
        /// Unique identifier for this particular continuation. Most useful for
components that
        /// retrieve the continuation data via <see cref="GetContinuationArgs"/>
and need
        /// to perform their own replay check
        /// </summary>
        public Guid Id { get { return id; } }

        /// <summary>
        /// Retrieves the continuation args, optionally retrieving them even if
they have already
        /// been retrieved
        /// </summary>
        /// <param name="includeStaleArgs">Set to true to return args even if they
have previously been returned</param>
        /// <returns>The continuation args or null if there aren't any</returns>
        public IContinuationActivatedEventArgs GetContinuationArgs(bool
includeStaleArgs)
        {
            if (!includeStaleArgs && handled)
                return null;
            MarkAsStale();
            return args;
        }
    }

    /// <summary>
    /// Implement this interface if your page invokes the file open picker
    /// API
    /// </summary>
    interface IFileOpenPickerContinuable
    {
```

```csharp
        /// <summary>
        /// This method is invoked when the file open picker returns picked
        /// files
        /// </summary>
        /// <param name="args">Activated event args object that contains returned
files from file open picker</param>
        void ContinueFileOpenPicker(FileOpenPickerContinuationEventArgs args);
    }


    /// <summary>
    /// Implement this interface if your page invokes the file save picker
    /// API
    /// </summary>
    interface IFileSavePickerContinuable
    {
        /// <summary>
        /// This method is invoked when the file save picker returns saved
        /// files
        /// </summary>
        /// <param name="args">Activated event args object that contains returned
file from file save picker</param>
        void ContinueFileSavePicker(FileSavePickerContinuationEventArgs args);
    }


    /// <summary>
    /// Implement this interface if your page invokes the folder picker API
    /// </summary>
    interface IFolderPickerContinuable
    {
        /// <summary>
        /// This method is invoked when the folder picker returns the picked
        /// folder
        /// </summary>
        /// <param name="args">Activated event args object that contains returned
folder from folder picker</param>
        void ContinueFolderPicker(FolderPickerContinuationEventArgs args);
    }


    /// <summary>
    /// Implement this interface if your page invokes the web authentication
    /// broker
    /// </summary>
    interface IWebAuthenticationContinuable
    {
        /// <summary>
        /// This method is invoked when the web authentication broker returns
        /// with the authentication result
        /// </summary>
        /// <param name="args">Activated event args object that contains returned
authentication token</param>
        void ContinueWebAuthentication(WebAuthenticationBrokerContinuationEventArgs
args);
    }

#endif
```

The purpose of this class is to make the suspension process transparent to the developer. It will take care of managing the activation event, redirecting the user to the page that invoked the **FileOpenPicker** and giving access to the file selected by the user.

Once you've added the **ContinuationManager** class to the project, it's time to change the **App** class configuration. The first step to do so is to create a new instance of the class in the **App** constructor, like in the following sample:

```csharp
public sealed partial class App : Application
{
    public static ContinuationManager ContinuationManager { get; private set; }

    public App()
    {
        this.InitializeComponent();
        this.Suspending += this.OnSuspending;
        ContinuationManager = new ContinuationManager();
    }
}
```

The next steps are to properly manage the activating and suspending events, since they're the ones that are involved when you use the **FileOpenPicker** in Windows Phone. When the picker is activated, the app is suspended. After the user has chosen the file, the app is reactivated and it contains the selected file in the activation parameters.

The following sample shows how to properly manage the **OnActivated()** method of the **App** class by using the **ContinuationManager**:

```csharp
protected override void OnActivated(IActivatedEventArgs args)
{
    if (args.Kind == ActivationKind.PickFileContinuation)
    {
        var continuationEventArgs = args as IContinuationActivatedEventArgs;
        if (continuationEventArgs != null)
        {
            ContinuationManager.Continue(continuationEventArgs);
            ContinuationManager.MarkAsStale();
        }
    }
}
```

The most important activation events (like the ones related to some contracts or extensions) are managed with a specific method. However, the **App** class also offers a generic method that is triggered for all the activation events that are not covered with a specific one. The **FileOpenPicker** activation is one of them, so we need to manage the generic **OnActivated()** event. The method's parameter contains a property called **Kind** which describes the activation event that triggered it by using one of the values of the **ActivationKind** enumerator. In our scenario, we need to manage the **PickFileContinuation** value. In this case, we can use the **ContinuationManager** by first calling the **Continue()** method (passing as parameter the activation arguments) and then the **MarkAsStale()** one. The **Continue()** method is the key of the operation; it redirects the user to the original page that invoked the picker UI, carrying as parameter the chosen file. The **MarkAsStale()** one, instead, is used to mark the current data as obsolete. This way, we make sure that the next usages of the **FileOpenPicker** won't return old data. For the same reason, we need to call the **MarkAsStale()** method also in the **OnSuspending()** method. This way, when the app is suspended due to a **FileOpenPicker** usage, we make sure that the old data is gone. Here is how to properly manage the **OnSuspending()** method:

```
private void OnSuspending(object sender, SuspendingEventArgs e)
{
    ContinuationManager.MarkAsStale();
}
```

We've completed the work on the **App** class. The **Continue()** method of the **ContinuationManager** class will redirect the user to the page that invoked the picker so we need to move the code behind the class of that page. The first step to do this is to implement a special interface which is declared in the **ContinuationManager** class. It's called **IFileOpenPickerContinuable** and it will require us to implement the **ContinueFileOpenPicker()** method. Here is a full sample:

```
public sealed partial class MainPage : Page, IFileOpenPickerContinuable
{
    public MainPage()
    {
        this.InitializeComponent();
    }

    public async void ContinueFileOpenPicker(FileOpenPickerContinuationEventArgs args)
    {
        StorageFile file = args.Files.FirstOrDefault();
        if (file != null)
        {
            var stream = await file.OpenReadAsync();
            BitmapImage image = new BitmapImage();
            await image.SetSourceAsync(stream);
            SelectedImage.Source = image;
        }
    }
}
```

The **ContinueFileOpenPicker()** method will allow us to complete our operation. The method's parameter contains a collection called **Files**, which is a list of files that have been selected in the picker by the user. The collection can contain just one file (in case you've used the **PickSingleFileAndContinue()** method) or it can contain more than one file (in case you've used the **PickMultipleFilesAndContinue()** method). The previous sample code manages a scenario in which the user can select an image using the picker. The selected image is retrieved in the **ContinueFileOpenPicker()** method and displayed to the user by using an **Image** control.

Importing a folder in Windows Phone uses the same approach. You're going to use the **FolderOpenPicker** class which offers a method called **PickFolderAndContinue()**; this triggers the suspension of the app and the picker UI opening:

```
private void OnPickFolderClicked(object sender, RoutedEventArgs e)
{
    FolderPicker picker = new FolderPicker();
    picker.FileTypeFilter.Add("*");
    picker.PickFolderAndContinue();
}
```

As we previously did for files, we now need to properly manage the **OnActivated()** method in the **App** class. This time, the **ActivationKind**'s value we are looking for is called **PickFolderContinuation**. In this case, as we did before, we're going to call the **Continue()** and the **MarkAsStale()** methods of the **ContinuationManager** so that the user can be redirect to the page that invoked the picker UI:

```
protected override void OnActivated(IActivatedEventArgs args)
{
    if (args.Kind == ActivationKind.PickFolderContinuation)
    {
        var continuationEventArgs = args as IContinuationActivatedEventArgs;
        if (continuationEventArgs != null)
        {
            ContinuationManager.Continue(continuationEventArgs);
            ContinuationManager.MarkAsStale();
        }
    }
}
```

The last step is to implement, in the code behind of the page that invoked the **FolderOpenPicker**, the **IFolderPickerContinuable** interface. This will require us to implement the **ContinueFolderPicker** method; it's the one that will receive, as parameter, the selected folder. The following sample shows how to retrieve the selected folder (thanks to the **Folder** property) and display to the user the name of all the files stored in it:

```
public sealed partial class MainPage : Page, IFolderPickerContinuable
{
    public MainPage()
    {
        this.InitializeComponent();
    }
```

```
public async void ContinueFolderPicker(FolderPickerContinuationEventArgs args)
{
    StorageFolder folder = args.Folder;
    if (folder != null)
    {
        var files = await folder.GetFilesAsync();
        foreach (StorageFile file in files)
        {
            MessageDialog dialog = new MessageDialog(file.DisplayName);
            await dialog.ShowAsync();
        }
    }
}
```

Accessing Files Stored on External Memory

Many tablets and smartphones offer a way to expand the internal storage memory by using a Secure Digital (SD) card or external Universal Serial Bus (USB) memory. The approach to access files and folders stored on external memory relies on the same concepts previously explained in this chapter, such as using the **StorageFolder** and **StorageFile** classes. However, there's an important difference to keep in mind: you can't freely access any file stored in the memory; you can only read and write files (whose type has been declared in the manifest file).

Consequently, the first step is to register the extensions we want to manage. We can do this in the **Declarations** section of the manifest file. We need to add a new **File Type Association** element which is available in the **Available declarations** drop-down menu. To work properly, this extension requires the following settings:

- A unique name that identifies the extension registration, which needs to be set in the **Name** field
- The file extensions we want to support. For each of them, we need to specify the **File Type** field (which is the extension such as .txt) and, optionally, the **Content Type** field (for example, in the case of a text plain, it's text/plain)

Now we are able to access all the files whose extensions have been specified in the manifest file. We can do this thanks to the **KnownFolders** class which is a static class that offers quick access to all of the device's libraries. We will talk about this again in Chapter 9 when we learn how to access the multimedia libraries. One of these libraries is called **RemovableDevices**, which is a **StorageFolder** object that provides access to the removable devices.

It's important to keep in mind that a Windows device can have multiple removable devices (for example, a tablet with a USB memory and a SD card slot) or no removable devices at all (such as a smartphone without a SD card slot). Every device is treated as a folder. To discover all of the available removable memories, we need to call the `GetFoldersAsync()` method on the `RemovableDevices` class. The following sample code shows a typical scenario for a Windows Phone app. We first get the list of all of the available devices and, if the number of results is greater than zero, it means that the phone supports external memory. Only in this case, we get the list of all of the available files stored in the first memory (since a smartphone can't have more than one SD card slot). We display it to the user by using a `ListView` control:

```
private async void OnGetFilesClicked(object sender, RoutedEventArgs e)
{
    StorageFolder card = KnownFolders.RemovableDevices;
    IReadOnlyList<StorageFolder> folders = await card.GetFoldersAsync();
    if (folders.Count > 0)
    {
        IReadOnlyList<StorageFile> files = await folders[0].GetFilesAsync();
        FilesList.ItemsSource = files;
    }
}
```

It's important to remember that, in this sample, the `GetFilesAsync()` method won't return all of the files stored in the external memory; it will only return the files whose extension matches the one we've declared in the manifest file. In this sample, it would return only the text files, which extension is .txt.

Testing SD Card Support in a Windows Phone App

Testing a Windows Phone app against the SD card support isn't always an easy task, since not all of the devices on the market offer external memory support. For this reason, the Windows Phone emulator is able to simulate the SD card so that we can test that our code is able to properly read and write files on an external memory.

This tool is included in the emulator's **Additional tools** and it simply requires us to choose a folder on our computer (which will be plugged into the emulator and treated as if it's an SD card). It's important to highlight that, by enabling this feature, the selected folder won't become a fake SD card but, rather, its content will just be copied inside the emulator. Consequently, if you execute some code that, for example, creates a new file on the SD card, you won't immediately find it in the folder. You'll need to enable the option called "Sync updated files back to the local folder when the SD card is ejected" and then press **Eject** to simulate the SD card removal. This way, the content of the emulator's SD card will copied back to the original folder so that you can check that your code executed with success.

Managing the App's Data

So far, we've learned how to manage the different storages that Windows and Windows Phone offer to developers, and how we can easily create and read files and folders. However, the most important requirement when it comes to managing local data is saving them in a more structured way so that it's easier to perform the most common operations (such as adding, removing, or editing an item).

Let's say that we want to develop an app that needs to manage a list of customers. We can't simply write this information into a text file since it would be hard to create a logical connection between the data and to perform simple queries (such as retrieving the list of all of the customers or adding a new one). Let's take a look at the best techniques with which to manage this scenario.

Serialization and Deserialization

Serialization is the simplest way to store the app's data in the local storage. This process makes it possible to store complex data (such as objects) into plain text files which can be easily saved in storage. The most common standards used for this scenario are XML and JSON. Deserialization is simply the opposite approach: the plain data is converted back into complex objects which can be easily manipulated by the app.

Serialization is made easier by the Windows Runtime since it offers a set of built-in classes that are able to automatically perform these operations. We won't have to manually write the XML or the JSON file that matches our data since the Runtime will take care of it for us. Usually, the serialization is performed every time the data is modified (for example, when an item is added, edited, or deleted) so that we can minimize the data loss risk in case of unexpected problems with the apps. Deserialization, instead, is performed when the app is opened or restored from a suspension.

Let's take a look at a serialization sample in which we'll use a simple class to describe a person. In the app, we're going to store a list of people:

```
public class Person
{
    public string Name { get; set; }
    public string Surname { get; set; }
}
```

In a typical app, we're going to work with a collection of data which can be retrieved, for example, from a web service or from a database. In the following sample, we're going to create a sample set of data:

```
public sealed partial class MainPage : Page
{
    private List<Person> people;

    public MainPage()
    {
```

```
        this.InitializeComponent();
    }

    protected override void OnNavigatedTo(NavigationEventArgs e)
    {
        people = new List<Person>
        {
            new Person
            {
                Name = "Matteo",
                Surname = "Pagani"
            },
            new Person
            {
                Name = "Ugo",
                Surname = "Lattanzi"
            }
        };
    }
}
```

Serializing and Deserializing Data by Using XML

Since the serialization is performed using a text file, we're going to use the previously described APIs to create a XML file in the local storage. The following sample creates a file called **people.xml** in the local storage by using the **CreateFileAsync()** and **OpenAsync()** methods that we've previously seen:

```
private async void OnSerializeDataClicked(object sender, RoutedEventArgs e)
{
    DataContractSerializer serializer = new
DataContractSerializer(typeof(List<Person>));
    StorageFile file = await ApplicationData.Current.LocalFolder.
    CreateFileAsync("people.xml", CreationCollisionOption.ReplaceExisting);
    IRandomAccessStream randomAccessStream = await file.OpenAsync(FileAccessMode.
    ReadWrite);
    using (Stream stream = randomAccessStream.AsStreamForWrite())
    {
        serializer.WriteObject(stream, people);
        await stream.FlushAsync();
    }
}
```

The XML serialization and deserialization process is performed by using the **DataContractSerializer** class which is part of the **System.Runtime.Serialization** namespace. When we create a new instance of this class, we need to specify the data type we're going to save; in our sample, it's **List<Person>**.

Next, as we've previously seen in this chapter, we create a new file called **people.xml**. We open the writing stream by using the **AsStreamForWrite()** method on the **IRandomAccessStream** object. The serialization procedure is performed by using the **WriteObject()** method of the **DataContractSerializer** class, which requires the destination stream (the file we've just created) and the data that we want to serialize (the collection of **Person** objects). In the end, we call the **FlushAsync()** method which forces all of the data that is still in the buffer to be written in the stream.

If you check the content of your local storage, you'll find a file called **people.xml** with the following content, which is a plain representation of our data:

```xml
<?xml version="1.0" encoding="utf-8" ?>
<ArrayOfPerson xmlns="http://schemas.datacontract.org/2004/07/StorageWin8"
xmlns:i="http://www.w3.org/2001/XMLSchema-instance">
  <Person>
    <Name>Matteo</Name>
    <Surname>Pagani</Surname>
  </Person>
  <Person>
    <Name>Ugo</Name>
    <Surname>Lattanzi</Surname>
  </Person>
</ArrayOfPerson>
```

The opposite process (which is the deserialization) is a very similar one since it's always performed by using the **DataContractSerializer** class. The differences is that, this time, we just need a reading stream, which is passed as parameter of the **ReadObject()** method offered by the **DataContractSerializer** class. Let's look at the following sample:

```csharp
private async void OnDeserializeClicked(object sender, RoutedEventArgs e)
{
    StorageFile file = await
ApplicationData.Current.LocalFolder.GetFileAsync("people.xml");
    DataContractSerializer serializer = new
DataContractSerializer(typeof(List<Person>));
    IRandomAccessStream randomAccessStream = await
file.OpenAsync(FileAccessMode.Read);
    List<Person> people = new List<Person>();
    using (Stream stream = randomAccessStream.AsStreamForRead())
    {
        people = serializer.ReadObject(stream) as List<Person>;
    }
}
```

After getting a reference to the **people.xml** file by using the **GetFileAsync()** method and opening the read stream by using the **AsStreamForRead()** method, we call the **ReadObject()** method that returns a generic object. It's our duty to perform a cast so that we can get back the data type we expect (in our case, it's a **List<People>** collection).

Serializing and Deserializing by Using JSON

The Windows Runtime also offers a way to serialize the data by using the JSON format, which has a shorter syntax and, consequently, requires less space to store. To work with the JSON format, we can use the same exact code we've previously seen by using XML. The only difference is that, instead of the **DataContractSerializer** class, we're going to use the **DataContractJsonSerializer** one. Let's take a look at the following sample:

```
private async void OnSerializeDataClicked(object sender, RoutedEventArgs e)
{
    DataContractJsonSerializer serializer = new
DataContractJsonSerializer(typeof(List<Person>));
    StorageFile file = await ApplicationData.Current.LocalFolder.
CreateFileAsync("people.json", CreationCollisionOption.ReplaceExisting);
    IRandomAccessStream randomAccessStream = await file.OpenAsync(FileAccessMode.
ReadWrite);
    using (Stream stream = randomAccessStream.AsStreamForWrite())
    {
        serializer.WriteObject(stream, people);
        await stream.FlushAsync();
    }
}
```

As you can see, there are no differences except for the serialization class we're using. The **WriteObject()** method will produce the following JSON file:

```
[
    {
        "Name":"Matteo",
        "Surname":"Pagani"
    },
    {
        "Name":"Ugo",
        "Surname":"Lattanzi"
    }
]
```

Here is how we can perform deserialization:

```
private async void OnDeserializeClicked(object sender, RoutedEventArgs e)
{
    StorageFile file = await
ApplicationData.Current.LocalFolder.GetFileAsync("people.json");
    DataContractJsonSerializer serializer = new
DataContractJsonSerializer(typeof(List<Person>));
    IRandomAccessStream randomAccessStream = await
file.OpenAsync(FileAccessMode.Read);
    List<Person> people = new List<Person>();
    using (Stream stream = randomAccessStream.AsStreamForRead())
    {
        people = serializer.ReadObject(stream) as List<Person>;
```

```
        }
}
```

Controlling the Serialization

By default, all of the properties that belong to a class are automatically serialized when we use the `DataContractSerializer` or the `DataContractJsonSerializer` classes. However, there are some scenarios in which we would like to avoid serializing one or more properties (for example, if they contain binary data such as an image so they can't be properly serialized).

To achieve this goal, the Windows Runtime offers a set of attributes that we can use to decorate our class, like in the following sample:

```
[DataContract]
public class Person
{
    [DataMember]
    public string Name { get; set; }

    [DataMember]
    public string Surname { get; set; }

    public BitmapImage Photo { get; set; }
}
```

First, we've added a `DataContract` attribute to the whole class. Then, we've added a `DataMember` attribute to every property we want to serialize; all of the others will be ignored. In the previous sample, only the `Name` and `Surname` properties will be serialized. The `Photo` property (which type is `BitmapImage` and can't be serialized) will be ignored.

Using a Database: SQLite

Serialization is easy to use but it also has some limitations. The most important limitation it has is that all of the data needs to be stored in memory. Since we can't manipulate the data directly, we first need to deserialize the entire collection in memory before we can perform any operation on it. In addition, serialization doesn't play well when you have a lot of data with relationships between them (for example, when you don't have to manage just a collection of people but also a collection of orders made by these people).

Databases are the best technology for these scenarios. By using databases, we are able to keep all of the data in the storage and retrieve only the subset that we need (thanks to queries). In addition, we are also able to create relationships between the data so that we can easily retrieve, for example, all of the orders made by a specific person.

Unlike Windows Phone 8.0 (which also offers native support to a database by using a Microsoft technology called SQL CE), Windows Phone 8.1 only relies on SQLite, a third-party technology for database support. SQLite offers the following advantages:

- It's a widely used open-source project that is supported by many companies such as Adobe, Oracle, and Nokia.
- It's able to work as a disconnected database engine. Unlike traditional database solutions such as SQL Server (which requires a special service called a Database Management System, or DBMS, to act as a middleman between the data and the apps), SQLite databases are plain binary files which can be directly accessed from the client app.
- It's cross-platform; you'll find a SQLite implementation for a lot of platform, both mobile (Windows Phone, Windows, iOS, Android, etc.) and traditional (desktop apps, web apps, etc.)
- It's written in C++ which provides great performance.

Since SQLite is a third-party database, you won't find it included in the Windows Runtime. You'll have to install the SQLite engine separately.

Installing the SQLite Engine

The first step to start using SQLite in your Windows Store apps is to install the engine, which is available as a Visual Studio extension. There are two different extensions to install: one for Windows 8.1 here and one for Windows Phone 8.1 here.

Once you've installed the extensions, you'll find them in the Add Reference menu, which is displayed when you right-click a project in Solution Explorer. If it's a Windows project, you'll have to look for the engine in the **Windows 8.1 – Extensions** section; it's called "SQLite for Windows Runtime (Windows 8.1)". If it's a Windows Phone project instead, you'll have to look for it in the **Windows Phone 8.1 – Extensions** section; it's called "SQLite for Windows Runtime (Windows Phone 8.1)". Before moving on, there's an important change to apply. If you try to build your project after adding the engine, you'll get a compilation error, which will state that the current architecture is not supported by the SQLite engine.

This is the downside of adding a C++ library to your project as native libraries can't be compiled with the standard **Any CPU** configuration (which is used to create apps that are able to run either on x86, x64, or ARM devices). This means that we'll need to change the configuration of our project to compile a specific package for each architecture. When we submit the app on the Store, we'll have to submit all of the packages, and the Store will take care of offering to the user the most appropriate one for their device. This approach applies specifically to Windows apps, which can run both on x86 and x64 devices (such as computers) and on ARM devices (such as tablets). Windows Phone doesn't suffer from this problem since you can find only ARM devices on the market.

To solve this problem, you'll need to open the **Configuration manager** window which is available in the Build menu. Now, in the drop-down menu called **Active Solution platform**, you'll need to choose the most appropriate configuration for your requirements. If you're testing your app on a computer or on the Windows Phone emulator, you'll have to choose X86 or X64. If you're testing your app on an ARM tablet or on a Windows Phone device, you'll have to choose ARM.

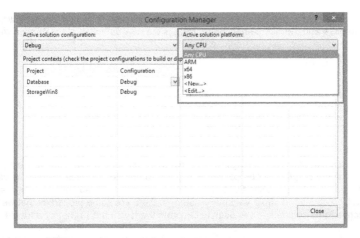

Figure 8: The Configuration Manager window

Performing Operations on the Database: SQLite-net

In the previous step, what we installed was just the SQLite engine. However, without additional support, the only way we would have to perform operations on a database is to write C++ code, which is not so straightforward. In fact, if you're reading this book, it's more likely that you know C# or VB.NET. Consequently, some third-party developers have created a set of additional libraries that can help developers to perform operations on a database by using a high-level language such as C#.

Third-party developer Frank A. Krueger has created one of these libraries called SQLite-net. It's an open-source project hosted on GitHub here and it's available as a NuGet package here. If you've ever worked with SQL CE on Windows Phone 8.0, you'll find this approach familiar. In fact, SQLite-net offers a LINQ-based approach similar to the one offered by libraries such as LINQ to SQL or Entity Framework. These libraries are called Object-Relational Mapping (ORM) and act as a middleman between the database and the app. Instead of forcing the developer to think about the app's data in two different ways (that is, classes and objects in the code, and columns and rows in the database), it takes care of it for them by automatically translating operations on objects (such as adding an item to a collection) in queries that are performed on the database.

Creating a Database

The approach used by SQLite-net to work with a SQLite database is called code-first. We'll be able to apply some special attributes to our classes in the code, which will tell the SQLite engine how to translate them in tables, rows, and columns. The first time that the app will be launched, the database will be created in the local storage by using the following conventions:

- Entities are converted into tables
- Properties are converted into columns
- Items are converted into rows

The following sample shows how to manage, again, a collection of people, this time with a SQLite database and the SQLite-net library. Here is the new definition of the **Person** class:

```
public class Person
{
    [PrimaryKey, AutoIncrement]
    public int Id { get; set; }
    [MaxLength(30)]
    public string Name { get; set; }
    public string Surname { get; set; }
}
```

By default, SQLite-net will create a table in the database with the same name of the class. Additionally, every property will be converted into a column with the same name. The column's type will be automatically detected based upon the property's type (so, for example, a **string** property will be converted into a **varchar** column). If there are some properties that we don't want to convert into columns, it's enough to decorate them with the **[Ignore]** attribute.

SQLite-net also offers a set of additional attributes that can be used to customize the table generation. In the previous sample, you saw some of them including **[PrimaryKey]** and **[AutoIncrement]**, which have been applied to the **Id** field to specify that it's the primary key of the table and that it's value will be auto-generated. You also saw **[MaxLength]** which is useful for optimizing performance by setting the maximum length of the string that can be stored in the column.

Once we've defined our database schema, we are ready to create it and perform the operations. The heart of the SQLite-net library is the **SQLiteAsyncConnection** class. Here is how we can use it to create the database when the app is launched:

```
private async void OnCreateDatabaseClicked(object sender, RoutedEventArgs e)
{
    SQLiteAsyncConnection conn = new
SQLiteAsyncConnection(Path.Combine(ApplicationData.Current.LocalFolder.Path,
"people.db"), true);
    await conn.CreateTableAsync<Person>();
}
```

The parameter required when we create a new instance of the **SQLiteAsyncConnection** object is the name and path of the database with which we want to work. In the previous sample, we're working with a file called **people.db** stored in the local storage's root. Then, for each table we want to create, we need to call the **CreateTableAsync<T>()** method where T is the type of data we want to store. If the table already exists, the method will simply do nothing. Consequently, we can safely call it every time the app starts and the existing data won't be erased.

Performing Common Operations

The most common operation that you can perform with a database is inserting a new row into the table. We can do this by using the **InsertAsync()** method offered by the **SQLiteAsyncConnection** class, like in the following sample:

```
private async void OnInsertDataClicked(object sender, RoutedEventArgs e)
{
    SQLiteAsyncConnection conn = new
SQLiteAsyncConnection(Path.Combine(ApplicationData.Current.LocalFolder.Path,
"people.db"), true);
    Person person = new Person
    {
        Name = "Matteo",
        Surname = "Pagani"
    };
    await conn.InsertAsync(person);
}
```

As you can see, SQLite-net will take care of converting an object into a row for you. You'll simply have to pass, to the **InsertAsync()** method, the object you want to store in the database. From the object's type (in this case, **Person**), SQLite-net will automatically understand the correct table to which to store the data.

To retrieve the data, we can use the familiar LINQ methods applied to the **Table<T>** property offered by the **SQLiteAsyncConnection** object, where T is the data type with which we're working. The following sample shows how to use the **Where()** LINQ method to retrieve all of the people whose name is Matteo:

```
private async void OnReadDataClicked(object sender, RoutedEventArgs e)
{
    SQLiteAsyncConnection conn = new
SQLiteAsyncConnection(Path.Combine(ApplicationData.
    Current.LocalFolder.Path, "people.db"), true);
    var query = conn.Table<Person>().Where(x => x.Name == "Matteo");
    var result = await query.ToListAsync();
    foreach (Person item in result)
    {
        Debug.WriteLine(string.Format("{0}: {1} {2}", item.Id, item.Name,
item.Surname));
    }
}
```

The only difference with a standard LINQ operation is that calling the **Where()** method just prepares the query; to effectively perform the operation and get the list of results, we need to call the **ToListAsync()** method.

Update operations are performed by using another method of the **SQLiteAsyncConnection** class which is called **UpdateAsync()**. However, before using it, we first need to retrieve (using the previous approach) the item we want to modify, so that we can pass it to the update method, like in the following sample:

```
private async void OnUpdateDataClicked(object sender, RoutedEventArgs e)
{
    SQLiteAsyncConnection conn = new
SQLiteAsyncConnection(Path.Combine(ApplicationData.
    Current.LocalFolder.Path, "people.db"), true);
```

```
    Person person = await conn.Table<Person>().Where(x => x.Name ==
"Matteo").FirstOrDefaultAsync();
    person.Name = "Ugo";
    await conn.UpdateAsync(person);
}
```

After retrieving all of the people whose name is Matteo, we get a reference to the first one of the list by using the **FirstOrDefaultAsync()** method. Then, after changing the person's name, we pass the retrieved object to the **UpdateAsync()** method to perform the operation.

The insert and update operations can also be performed with multiple items by using the **InsertAll()** and **UpdateAll()** methods, which accepts a collection of objects instead of just a single one.

Finally, if you want to delete an existing item, you need to call the **DeleteAsync()** method offered by the **SQLiteAsyncConnection** class. Again, you'll have to first get a reference to the item you want to delete so that you can pass it to the **DeleteAsync()** method, like in the following sample:

```
private async void OnDeleteDataClicked(object sender, RoutedEventArgs e)
{
    SQLiteAsyncConnection conn = new
SQLiteAsyncConnection(Path.Combine(ApplicationData.
    Current.LocalFolder.Path, "people.db"), true);
    Person person = await conn.Table<Person>().Where(x => x.Name ==
"Matteo").FirstOrDefaultAsync();
    await conn.DeleteAsync(person);
}
```

SQLite-net: Pros and Cons

Similar to every other tool, SQLite-net has its pros and cons. For sure, the biggest SQLite-net pro is its simplicity. Thanks to the LINQ approach, we can easily use a database even if we're not very familiar with the SQL syntax.

SQLite-net's biggest con is that the library isn't 100 percent complete since it doesn't support all of the scenarios that a relational database can manage. The most important scenario are relationships; SQLite-net doesn't offer a way to create a relationship between tables and to define foreign keys. Consequently, we don't have an easy way to perform a query that is able to retrieve related data from two or more tables. The only viable approach is to perform multiple nested queries; those, however, have a negative impact on performance.

Portable Class Library for SQLite

Microsoft (through the Microsoft Open Technologies subsidiary) has created a library called **Portable Class Library for SQLite**, which offers a completely different approach than SQLite-net. Instead of providing a middle layer that translates operations on objects in SQL queries, it gives maximum flexibility to the developer. You'll be able to interact with the database as you would do with a traditional app, by manually writing the SQL queries needed to perform the operations. We won't talk in detail about the SQL statements we'll describe in this chapter since it's out of scope for this book; I'll just assume that you have a basic knowledge of SQL.

You can install this library to your project using NuGet here.

Creating the Database

Since, in this case, there's no middle layer that translates the code in query for us, we won't have to set up any mapping between classes and tables. To create a table, we will just perform a **CREATE TABLE** query, like in the following sample:

```
private void OnCreateDatabaseClicked(object sender, RoutedEventArgs e)
{
    using (SQLiteConnection conn = new SQLiteConnection("people.db"))
    {
        string query = "CREATE TABLE IF NOT EXISTS PEOPLE " +
        "(Id INTEGER PRIMARY KEY AUTOINCREMENT NOT NULL," +
        "Name varchar(100), " +
        "Surname varchar(100))";
        ISQLiteStatement statement = conn.Prepare(query);
        statement.Step();
    }
}
```

The connection is created by using the **SQLiteConnection** object, which requires as parameter the name of the file with which we want to work (in this case, it's called **people.db**). By wrapping the connection inside a using statement, we make sure that, when the operation on the database is completed, we close the connection.

In the previous sample, we first define a simple string with the query to perform. Then we prepare it and turn it into a **ISQLiteStatement** object by calling the **Prepare()** method. In the end, we execute the query by calling the **Step()** method on the statement. Notice that, to the **CREATE TABLE** command, we've added the **IF NOT EXISTS** option. This way, we'll be able to run the query multiple times without issues. If the table already exists, the query simply won't be executed.

Performing Common Operations

To perform common operations using SQL, we need to introduce a new concept: parameters. In fact, SQLite supports a way to add parameters to a query so that some values can be defined at run time. The following sample shows how to use this approach to insert some data to the table we've previously created:

```
private void OnInsertDataClicked(object sender, RoutedEventArgs e)
```

```
{
    using (SQLiteConnection conn = new SQLiteConnection("people.db"))
    {
        using (var statement = conn.Prepare("INSERT INTO People (Name, Surname)
VALUES(@Name, @Surname);"))
        {
            statement.Bind("@Name", "Matteo");
            statement.Bind("@Surname", "Pagani");
            statement.Step();

            statement.Reset();
            statement.ClearBindings();
            statement.Bind("@Name", "Ugo");
            statement.Bind("@Surname", "Lattanzi");
            statement.Step();
        }
    }
}
```

The basic approach is the same: we define a query and we turn it into an **ISQLiteStatement**
object by using the **Prepare()** method. However, this time, you will notice that we've added two
parameters to the query which are identified by the @ symbol: **@Name** and **@Surname**. Before
executing the query, we need to configure the statement so that it knows which values to assign
to these parameters. We do this by using the **Bind()** method which requires the parameter's
name and the value we want to assign. Only after we've performed this operation can we call
the **Step()** method to execute the query.

If we want to insert another item without creating a new **ISQLiteStatement** object, we can
reset the already existing one by calling the **Reset()** and the **ClearBindings()** methods. This
way, we can call the **Bind()** method again to assign new values to the parameters and then call
the **Step()** method to execute the query.

When it comes to reading data from a table, we're going to use the same approach, with one
difference: when you're retrieving some data from a table, you can get multiple rows as a result.
Consequently, the library will return you an iterator which we will need to process in order to get
all of the results. This goal is achieved using the same **Step()** method we've seen before; the
difference is that, this time, every time we'll call it, we'll get just one row in return. Therefore, we
will need to invoke it multiple times until all of the rows have been processed. Let's take a look
at the following sample:

```
private void OnReadDataClicked(object sender, RoutedEventArgs e)
{
    using (SQLiteConnection conn = new SQLiteConnection("people.db"))
    {
        using (var statement = conn.Prepare("SELECT * FROM People ORDER BY Name;"))
        {
            while (statement.Step() == SQLiteResult.ROW)
            {
                long id = (long)statement[0];
                string name = (string)statement[1];
                string surname = (string)statement[2];
                Debug.WriteLine("Id: {0} - Name: {1} - Surname: {2}", id, name,
```

```
surname);
        }
    }
}
}
```

After we've defined the query (which simply returns all of the rows stored in the People table, ordered by name), we turn it into a **ISQLiteStatement** object. Then we call the **Step()** method inside a **while** statement. This method returns the result's type of the query: if the value is **ROW**, it means that there are still rows to process. This **while** statement makes sure that the iteration is repeated until all of the rows have been processed.

For each single row, we are able to extract the data by using the **ISQLiteStatement** object and by treating it as an array; every array's position matches the table's columns. Therefore, in the previous sample, we can use the index 0 to retrieve the value of the column **Id** or the index 1 to retrieve the value of the column **Name**. However, the array contains generic objects so we need to perform a cast to the type we expect.

In the end, when it comes to updating or deleting the data, there are no new concepts to introduce; the approach is always the same. We prepare the query, we set the parameters, and we perform it by converting it into an **ISQLiteStatement** object. The following sample shows how to perform an update:

```
private void OnUpdateDataClicked(object sender, RoutedEventArgs e)
{
    using (SQLiteConnection conn = new SQLiteConnection("people.db"))
    {
        string query = "UPDATE People SET Name=@Name WHERE Id=@Id";
        using (var statement = conn.Prepare(query))
        {
            statement.Bind("@Name", "Ugo");
            statement.Bind("@Id", 1);
            statement.Step();
        }
    }
}
```

Here is, instead, how to perform a delete:

```
private void OnDeleteDataClicked(object sender, RoutedEventArgs e)
{
    using (SQLiteConnection conn = new SQLiteConnection("people.db"))
    {
        string query = "DELETE FROM People WHERE Id=@Id";
        using (var statement = conn.Prepare(query))
        {
            statement.Bind("@Id", 1);
            statement.Step();
        }
    }
}
```

Portable Class Library for SQLite: Pros and Cons

The biggest pro in using the Portable Class Library for SQLite is its flexibility: since you can write SQL statements, you'll be able to perform any operation that is supported by SQLite (such as managing indexes, relationships, etc.). However, this approach is more complex to use and makes the code harder to read since you will work with two different data approaches: tables, rows, and columns for the database, and objects and classes for the app. Consequently, you will need to manually convert from one data type to the other every time you need to perform an operation.

Using an Existing Database

There are many scenarios in which you don't need to start from scratch to create the database but where you already have a prepopulated one with some data. However, we can't simply add it to our project in Visual Studio and connect to it. If you remember what we learned in this chapter, the content of the project is copied into a read-only folder of the system. Because of this, we won't be able to perform any operation that alters the data in the database (such as adding a new item or editing an existing one).

Consequently, the best approach is to copy the database from the project to the local storage the first time the app is started. This way, since the database will be stored in the local storage, we will have both read and write access. Thanks to the knowledge we acquired in this chapter, it's easy to write a method that performs this operation:

```
private async Task CopyDatabase()
{
    bool isDatabaseExisting = false;
    try
    {
        StorageFile storageFile = await ApplicationData.Current.LocalFolder.
        GetFileAsync("people.db");
        isDatabaseExisting = true;
    }
    catch
    {
        isDatabaseExisting = false;
    }
    if (!isDatabaseExisting)
    {
        StorageFile databaseFile = await Package.Current.InstalledLocation.
        GetFileAsync("people.db");
        await databaseFile.CopyAsync(ApplicationData.Current.LocalFolder);
    }
}
```

In this sample, we assume that we have a file called **people.db** in our project. First, we check to see whether or not the file is already existing in the local storage by calling the `GetFileAsync()` method (and intercepting the exception that can be raised if the file doesn't exist).

Only if the database doesn't exist do we then copy it from the project by using the `Package.Current.InstalledLocation` class we previously mentioned in this chapter. The copy is performed by using the `CopyAsync()` method, which requires the destination folder as parameter (in this case, the local storage).

Exploring the Database Content

During the testing phase, we may be required to take a look at the data stored in the database in order to understand if everything is okay. There are many free and commercial tools available on the Internet that are able to open a SQLite database and perform queries on it. You can find a complete list on the official SQLite website here.

One of the best available tools (which comes both in a free and a paid version) is called SQLite Expert, which can be downloaded here.

Storing Sensitive Data

The Windows Runtime offers a set of classes specifically to help store sensitive data such as service credentials. These classes, which are part of the `Windows.Security.Credentials` namespace, are able to:

- Keep the data isolated so that they can't be accessed by other apps
- Encrypt the data
- Synchronize the data with all of the other devices registered with the same Microsoft Account and that have been marked as trusted

The key class to store sensitive data is called `PasswordVault`, which can store one or more `PasswordCredential` objects, like in the following sample:

```
private void OnSavePasswordClicked(object sender, RoutedEventArgs e)
{
    PasswordVault vault = new PasswordVault();
    PasswordCredential credential = new
PasswordCredential("YourServiceCredentials", "username", "password");
    vault.Add(credential);
}
```

Every credential is identified by a unique name, which is the first parameter passed to the class constructor (in the sample, it's **YourServiceCredentials**). Then, you can specify the username and the password to store. To add a `PasswordCredential` object to the vault, it's enough to call the `Add()` method.

To retrieve the stored credentials, you can use the `FindAllByResource()` method offered by the `PasswordVault` class; it will return a list of `PasswordCredential` objects that match the given resource name. Typically, you will get just one result since you can't have two credentials stored with the same name. The following sample retrieves the previously stored credentials and displays them to the user:

```
private async void OnGetPasswordClicked(object sender, RoutedEventArgs e)
{
    PasswordVault vault = new PasswordVault();
    IReadOnlyList<PasswordCredential> credentials =
vault.FindAllByResource("YourServiceCredentials");
    if (credentials.Count > 0)
    {
        PasswordCredential credential = credentials.FirstOrDefault();
        credential.RetrievePassword();
        string message = string.Format("Username: {0} - Password: {1}",
credential.UserName, credential.Password);
        MessageDialog dialog = new MessageDialog(message);
        await dialog.ShowAsync();
    }
}
```

The only thing to highlight here is that, before accessing to the **Password** property of the
PasswordCredential class, we need to call the **RetrievePassword()** method as a security
measure; otherwise, we won't be able to read its value.

www.ingramcontent.com/pod-product-compliance
Lightning Source LLC
Chambersburg PA
CBHW071248050326
40690CB00011B/2311